Breaking The Code of Silence Now!

From 18 women who decided to break free
from the things that have kept them bound

Breaking The Code of Silence, Now!
Copyright 2019 Sha'Meca Latai' Oliver
ISBN: ISBN-13: 978-0-9991524-1-6

Visionary: Sha'Meca Latai' Oliver
Building The Best You, LLC.
Cover Design & Layout by Wesley, Dreams Alive Production, LLC.
Editor: Sha'Meca Latai' Oliver

Dedication

Breaking The Code of Silence, Now! is dedicated to the person who needs to be set free. It is for the those who no longer want to be held hostage by experiences that have caused them to feel and live broken and bound. It is for the overcomer, underachiever, rejected, boldest, brightest, confident and not so confident individual. It is for anyone who is ready to own their power and share their truth. It is for the world of people who are a voice for those who have silenced themselves.

Every story is powerful, because it takes courage and faith to release what has caused pain, shame, doubt and disbelief. Each co-author has boldly said, "Yes" to themselves. Without reservation, they share their stories of truth, endurance, insight and lessons learned. These, no-holds-barred women unashamedly have used their voices that were once silent to break free from the things that have kept them bound. They have stood in the gap and have written their journeys together, by linking arms virtually, from around the nation. Their stories are the voices that provide other women with the opportunity to be healed, successful and to understand they are not alone. The courses of their lives have changed. They are also changing the trajectory of many lives as witnesses that our pasts do not dictate our futures.

We hope that each story gives you liberty in your own life. You can become greater than what you have been through! It's your time to speak!

Table of Contents

Introduction
Sha'Meca Latai' Oliver————————————————— 7

Chapter 1
The Power of Weakness ———————————————— 13
Tyra Lane-Kingsland

Chapter 2
Living Outside My Comfort Zone - Living My Best Life ———————— 21
Nicole Bowman-Smith

Chapter 3
Opening the Treasure Box ————————————————— 29
Chihuana Hunter

Chapter 4
My Beneficent P.O.P. (Privilege of Power)———————————— 39
Danielle Fee Vaughn

Chapter 5
It Was Already Purposed ———————————————— 47
DeShanta Hinton

Chapter 6

Why I Live and Love Differently ———————— 57
Lisa A. Matthews

Chapter 7

When I Decided Enough Was Enough ———————— 65
Melinda Chervil Cobb

Chapter 8

Plagued by Failure, You Will Never Amount to Anything! ———— 77
Fasting and Going From Glory to Glory

LaDonna Mitchell (Horne)

Chapter 9

You Are No Longer Welcome Here! ———————— 87
Veronica Howard

Chapter 10

She Said...No! ———————————————— 99

Patricia (Shay) Cosey

Chapter 11

Surviving: Miscarriage and Beyond ———————— 109
Regina Franklin

Chapter 12

And then the Morning Comes…Trust in the Rainbow ———— 119
Rev. Dr. Rene Minter

Chapter 13

Boom, Click & Dial Tone - God Carried Me ——————— 131
"Working the Win Within"
Shay Lewis Sisco

Chapter 14

Moving Forward: 12 Hours Later ————————————— 143
Sherie Billingslea

Chapter 15

Losing Myself While Loving Somebody Else ——————— 155
   I was taking away from me
Toi Dickson-Fuller

Chapter 16

Assassinated the Posture of Fear – Destiny Wins ———— 167
Dianne Raiford

Chapter 17

Speak Now —————————————————————————— 177
Vickie Mclean

Chapter 18

Started From The Bottom, Now I'm Here ——————— 185
Deona Hinton

Call-To-Action Are You Ready To Write? ——————— 207

Authors Directory ——————————————————————— 208

About The Visionary ———————————————————— 209

Introduction

By Sha'Meca Latai' Oliver

The "Root Coach," Girl Code Extraordinaire, Pastor, International Spokeswoman
and Visionary for Breaking The Code of Silence, Now!

Sometimes, one of the hardest things we can do is speak about the most painful things that we've experienced. At times, it feels much easier to shove our problems underneath a rug and act like they don't exist. And, that's not true. Our problems still exist until we handle them. Our unhandled issues are like cancer lying dormant in the human body. When something is dormant it means that it isn't dead. It still has life and the ability to affect the life we live. Just like cancer, our issues surface when something activates them. They invade the body, infecting the things that keep us functional and healthy, causing us to live dysfunctional and unhealthy lives.

Unhandled issues leave us broken, not able to function at our full capacity. We tend to experience feelings of anger, frustration, bitterness, insecurity, or we become timid, controlling and guarded. These feelings, emotions and behaviors are often displayed almost everywhere that we go. The question is why?

Many times, we don't desire to deal with our issues because they hurt, badly. We are afraid of being embarrassed, enduring additional hurt, feeling ashamed or being rejected. Sometimes, we don't want to manage our issues because we think that we might hurt those that we love; because sometimes

7

our problems are caused by those closest to us. So, we mature from being a child to an adult, broken. How do we break free?

We must deal with our issues until they no longer have the ability to infect and affect us. We do this by first acknowledging that we have an issue or issues. We discuss every emotion, feeling, concern and experience. Some days we will have to cry it out, scream, dance, laugh but, it's so important to get it out! This is truly when healing starts to take place. Though this process can be hard and tumultuous, it is worth handling because it liberates us. It will liberate you!

I am truly blessed by and proud of each co-author who made the decision to say, "Yes" to themselves and to *"Breaking The Code of Silence, Now!"* Because, in the African American community there is a "knowing" through our culture that we better not talk about our issues; especially, if it's going to bring any type of negative focus on the family. We are told that we better not tell what "such and such" did to us or them. We grow up thinking that if we expose our pain, our character would be diminished. And that this type of negligence will cause shame to our families and our ability to thrive in life will be unsuccessful. We hold ourselves accountable to keeping these secrets. Not realizing that harboring anything unhealthy keeps us bound. I've been there, silently fighting a fight that was never meant for me to battle.

As a child, daily, I worried tremendously over the pain and the afflictions that many of my family members endured. I was never told not to talk about it. It was an unsaid, "knowing" rule, that I shouldn't expose the things that were causing arguments, physical abuse, mental frustration, loneliness, bitterness and rejection in my family. I'm assuming, I didn't verbalize it because many times it was understood that a child should stay in a child's place. Therefore, it seemed as if I equated not dealing with certain issues, even into my adult years, by keeping my ears and eyes tuned to the dysfunction around me but, remaining silent. I realize I was a child learning poor behaviors from adults, who probably should have known better, but realizing that they didn't. Their own dysfunction was handled more like a norm. It was a vicious cycle that kept me bound and broken for a long time mainly because I could not help those that I loved to break free, and eventually, it hindered me from knowing how to rescue me.

I suffered from compulsive worrying. It felt like if I didn't worry about someone or something, I didn't care. This was definitely a taught reaction to other people's problems. Which of course, I learned that holding things in and not dealing with issues can cause depression, anxiety, anger and so many more mental and physical ailments. I remember being about fourteen/fifteen years old, crying almost daily and my cousin told me, "You're not fun anymore." That really struck a nerve, but it also, gave me fuel for fire. I told her that I wasn't trying to be "not fun." I knew that worrying silenced something in me. It caused me to hide the person I wanted to be. It had cause me to isolate myself from the world and not pursue things I desired. I knew I didn't want to be that way anymore. So, I began to pray and express my feelings/experiences, rhythmically, on paper through poetry. It started to heal me. I started to heal others. Writing began to be a part of my voice and my freedom. This was the starting point of me learning not to let what I could not control, have a hold on me.

Throughout my life I've used writing as way to relieve me of life's daily stressors. I also use the power of sharing my challenges with others by speaking about them in order to break the chains that tried to break me. I've learned, through many experiences that I do not have to be ashamed, feel insignificant or embarrassed for having a trial, because they truly make us stronger even though they do not feel good. I've also learned that sometimes I must be a voice, so that others can use theirs. I have learned that I can overcome whatever tries to disrupt my flow of sanity and that my story has a testimony that can help someone else.

"And they overcame him by the blood of the Lamb, and by the word of their testimony"
-Revelation 12:11 (KJV)

I am absolutely humbled and thankful for each story written and proud of each co-author for owning her power by sharing the truth of her pain in hopes to set someone else free. And, this freedom was not just intended for the reader, but also for the writer. I'm as equally excited that they decided to break their code of silence "Now!" Doing something that that you have never done and to be unsure of the outcome (good or indifferent) takes faith.

The bible states in Hebrews 11:1, "Now, faith is the substance of things hoped for the evidence of things not seen." Their decision to share their struggle was a faith move; a present moment decision in hopes that their expected outcome will be greater than what their pain did to them. I witnessed freedom and breakthroughs happen through the process of completing this book amongst the co-authors. There were moments we cried, prayed and cheered each other on! That's girl power! That's sisterhood! That's standing in the gap! Each woman became a key for courage. By writing her story, she supported the next by showing her that we do not have to do life alone, anymore! None of these women look like what they have been through.

May you see yourself in their stories. May experience your own freedom from their wisdom, knowledge and lessons learned. May you hear God's voice through each word and may it echo a sound that causes you to have the courage to break free from everything that has kept you bound; NOW!

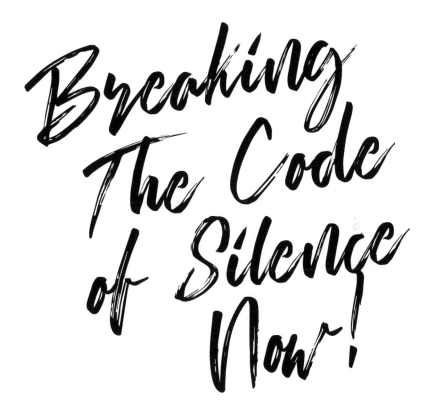

Breaking The Code of Silence Now!

From 18 women who decided to break free
from the things that have kept them bound

Breaking The Code of Silence, Now!

Chapter 1

The Power of Weakness

By Tyra Lane-Kingsland

"Weaknesses aren't flaws to be magnified but opportunities for God's grace to be glorified."

The Power of Weakness

"Whatever you want, whatever you need. Anything you want done baby, I'll do it naturally. 'Cause I'm every woman. It's all in me. It's all in me." You were singing it right along with me as you read the lyrics right? Whether your mind took you to Whitney or Chaka, you know this anthem. But do songs like these set us up for failure or for success. What if I'm not every woman? What if it's not all in me? What if I can't do everything and anything? What if attempting to do anything and everything causes me to break?

Be everything to everybody is what they tell you.

You're a strong Black woman is what they tell you.

Big Momma and 'nem had to deal with way much more;

you'll be fine, is what they say.

So you go ahead and keep up appearances.

You don't let them see you vulnerable.

You don't let them see you weak.

You don't let them see you make a mistake.

You put your best face on and smile through the tears and laugh through the pain.

That's what they tell us and that's what many of us do and yet it seems quite schizophrenic to me. Because you're only strong until you break. And all of us have our breaking point. You know the point at which you can't take any more pressure. Marriage pressure, children pressure, work pressure, the little girl in you that's screaming out for anyone to love her pressure. Sound familiar? Pressure to be assertive yet meek, to be friendly but not too nice lest someone take advantage of you, to set boundaries but not be "stuck-up". Too much pressure!

Yup, that was me until the pressure mounted so greatly that I broke. You see it's only so long before those hairline fractures give way and reveal true weakness. You ever see the tiniest little pebble hit the windshield and leave a microscope split? Have you known that same split to then travel the length of the windshield in a fraction of a second?

Here I was, like Atlas trying to hold up the sky, but I was buckling under the weight of the issues of life. If you could have caught a glimpse of me when the pot of rice on the stove was burning, the toddler was crying, helping three with homework also emailing the teacher about a missing assignment all the while pregnant with baby number six and was simply sick and tired of being *sick & tired*, you would have seen the crack that was about to turn into a full blown shatter.

Through it all I was thinking "I'm every woman and it's all in me". I tried to be strong; to be strong for my spouse, strong for the women I minister to, strong for my children, strong for my friends, strong for my Dad. I stuffed the tears and though they were right on the brink of falling out of my eyes I forced them back down. I told myself, *"Just pretend. Make everybody think everything is okay because you are ok right?"* Yeah right, I was NOT ok.

So, I kept pressing because life doesn't stop just because you're weak. Kids need to be raised, customers still expect me to show up and my man is still looking to get his special time with me. I forged ahead in my weakness because I heard that I can do all things through Christ who strengthens me. But I also know that the Word says when I am weak, His strength is made perfect.

And I was weak. I tried to live up to legacy of my ancestors who suffered atrocities I cannot imagine. And while those experiences of back breaking labor, rape, more are etched somewhere in my DNA and maybe I can dig way deep to draw on some of that strength, God has not given me those instructions.

But he said to me, "My grace is sufficient for you, for my power is made perfect in weakness." Therefore, I will boast all the more gladly about my weaknesses, so that Christ's power may rest on me. That is why, for Christ's sake, I delight in weaknesses, in insults, in hardships, in persecutions, in difficulties. For when I am weak, then I am strong. 2 Corinthians 12:9-10

So, the day finally came when I DECIDED I wasn't going to do it anymore. I wasn't going to "put on the Tyra." "Tyra" is exuberant, bubbly, effervescent, smiley, and encouraging. But this day I had had enough. I was not happy. In fact, I was downright sad, mentally exhausted and physically sick. My sixth pregnancy had taken a toll on my mind, my body and on my spirit. I was sick every single day all day. The weight of daily living was so heavy and I just couldn't carry it anymore.

A sweet gentle friend attempted to come to my aid and initially I tried to shut her down. No, I didn't want company. No, I don't want you to come see me right now in my robe and my hair in pin curls. Again, here's where trying to "be strong" and keep up appearances kills us softly on the inside. Did my friend care that I was in my robe with my hair in pin curls? NO! But I had created the backstory. The backstory said you only see Tyra when she's put together. You only speak to Tyra when she positive and upbeat. Well the dam broke that day because the friend came over anyway. Her sensitivity and perceptiveness caught wind of my heaviness and she extended to me God's invitation to lay my burdens at His feet. And while it was extremely embarrassing, even torturous for this prideful woman to admit I was a broken weak mess, it was one of the BEST things I've ever done. There was liberty in that place of weakness. It was in that place of weakness that God would teach me a powerful lesson.

The world says weakness, brokenness and vulnerability are imperfections, but God sees it as an opportunity to present you whole and blameless. He sees a chance to show Himself strong in and through you. Weakness gives you a divine appointment with God. It presents you with an opportunity to bring forth not just the you that dresses up and puts on makeup but also the you whose arms get tired. The you whose patience runs out. The you who has come to the end of herself yet has come to the beginning of resurrection POWER. It is there in that weak, vulnerable space that He will dwell with you.

For thus says the One who is high and lifted up, who inhabits eternity, whose name is Holy: "I dwell in the high and holy place, and also with him who is of a contrite and lowly spirit, to revive the spirit of the lowly, and to revive the heart of the contrite. Isaiah 57:15

Your brokenness before God is valuable. Kintsugi is a Japanese art form all about broken pieces. Dating back to the 15th century, it is a technique for repairing broken pottery. The word Kintsugi means "golden joinery". The process uses lacquer and real gold powder to fill in the cracks. The intricacy of the work involved, the precious materials used for the process and the skill of the repairers' hand, results in a mended work that is more valuable than the original product.

And this is what God wants to do for me and for you. When our arms are weak and we're trying to hold the pieces of our lives together, it's a loosely held bundle of shards at best but when we place the shards in the Potter's hands, He arranges, cements and then presents us even more beautiful than before.

Nellie Bly, an investigative journalist, did just that but for different reasons. In 1887 she wanted to uncover the horrors taking place at an asylum and the only way to get the real story was to become weak and broken, to act as if insane and have herself committed to the asylum. And she did just that. She was able to convince a judge and doctors that she was indeed broken. She did this for the greater good of the victims of this asylum. Her investigative reporting resulted in widespread changes in that asylum and in the field of mental health.

Are you willing to allow your weakness to be on display knowing it can possibly bring healing to another? The word says we overcome by the blood of the lamb and by the word of our testimony. Your testimony of weakness could be the catalyst not only for your own healing but for someone else's too. Just like He used Moses' weakness. Moses who was fearful and ran from his staff when it turned into a snake; God told him to PICK UP that very thing and use it as a sign. The very thing that Moses ran from was the same instrument that would hit a rock to bring water to nourish the people and would part the waters, so they could cross on dry land.

Being weak is part of the human experience. So, I have given myself permission to experience the full range of emotions and to partake in the depth and breadth of my personal experiences, knowing that perfect is an illusion. I'm learning to see the beauty in the mess-ups and weak moments. And I know he's using me right at my point of weakness. The people He's called me to share with don't want the carefully curated IG feed me, they want to real, mommy of 6, wife, and minister who done been through some thangs me.

In her book Daring Greatly, Dr. Brene Brown says, ***"To claim the truths about who we are, where we come from, what we believe, and the very imperfect nature of our lives, we have to be willing to give ourselves a break and appreciate the beauty of our cracks or imperfections."*** So how do you give yourself a break and allow your weakness to be on display? You put your foot down and declare that you love yourself enough to be free. You decide that you won't be held hostage to others' opinions of you. But it takes humility and vulnerability. This is a revolutionary act of courage. It takes true courage to say, "I'm tired. I'm lonely. I need a hug. I'm hurt, confused and overwhelmed."

Admitting you are weak breaks the code of silence and delivers you from pride, shame, insecurity, and false happiness. When you decide you don't give a crap what others think, you show up as you are. You give your authentic self, the one who was fearfully and wonderfully made in the beginning self, a chance to shine, weakness and all. This creates room for humility, vulnerability, security, healing, character transformation, freedom and joy. This is beautiful in the sight of God. It shows that you have not made yourself an idol and that you recognize your reliance of Him. When you have that recognition then you free the current of His power to flow through you.

How do you tap into this POWER? You start by receiving God's gift of grace. Grace is God's unmerited favor towards you. He seeks to lavish His grace upon you so that you have more than enough for whatever you set out to do (2 Corinthians 9:8). Next you must be gentle with yourself. We can be so hard on ourselves. We can set unrealistic expectation and sabotage ourselves. NO MORE! Embrace mistakes and imperfections as part of life's learning process. Human perfection is a fallacy. And finally identify a safe space where you can weak. Should that be in the arms of a loving friend, your spouse, alone in your prayer closet, at a worship service or even over your kitchen sink, have a place where you feel safe to unmask.

When you are weak His strength is made perfect. When you are weak, you become a conduit for God's perfect power to surge and flow through you. Are you weak? Sometimes the answer is yes and that's ok because weakness is your gateway to power!

Tyra Lane-Kingsland Bio

Tyra Lane-Kingsland is no stranger to inspiring hearts. From her role as a Women's Ministry Leader to her former role as a performance improvement coach and facilitator for a Top Twenty Fortune 500 Company, Tyra has provided encouragement to countless people. Her desire is to help women LIVE FULLY by nurturing the mind, body and spirit. Having been recognized as a Competent Communicator by Toastmasters International, Tyra is a sought-after speaker, blogger, coach and author of the book *Purposeful Parenting*. Tyra has written and facilitated courses on parenting and Health & Wellness. It is her assertion that health is wealth and that optimal health is achieved through proper nourishment, rest and exercise. Tyra is an attentive wife and mother of six. Having endured a tumultuous childhood but walking in victory today, Tyra knows first-hand that God trades beauty for ashes, joy for pain and a garment of praise for a spirit of heaviness. Knowing that God causes all things to work together for good, Tyra is on a passionate pursuit to see women inspired to live fully!

Chapter 2

Living Outside My Comfort Zone
Living my Best Life

By Nicole Bowman-Smith

"Feeling uncomfortable is a sign that you are not living your full potential."

Living Outside My Comfort Zone Living My Best Life

How did I find myself trapped inside of my comfort zone? I grew up seeing my parents and most of the people we associated with living comfortably. That is, they lived in a nice to decent house, they made comfortable money, drove nice cars and that was it. Now that I'm an adult, I've questioned if their comfortability was that just a front?

I watched my mom and dad go to work every day until they reach retirement age. They rarely went on vacations. They were not part of a social club and I never saw them doing anything outside of regular living. I do recall them hanging out with friends and family at cabarets and going out to night clubs. They would get dressed up and I sensed that they were excited about going. I wonder if they aspired to do anything other than work. I never asked because I thought what they were doing was normal. My mother tried to introduce us to various activities that I felt were forced upon us. Maybe these were some things she wanted to do in life. She wanted my sister and I to play the piano. We took private piano lessons and she bought a piano. I was not interested but, my sister showed a slight interest. Nothing significant came from that so, she took lessons herself. I believe my childhood led me to the comfort zone. I know I was hesitant to do anything outside of the normal because of my weight. I can remember all the things that made me uncomfortable.

I didn't go to the prom because I knew I would not have the perfect dress. We went dress shopping and the options were not what I envisioned as the perfect dress for prom and age appropriate. Everything in my size looked like mother of the bride dresses. Getting a dress made was not any option

22

that I even wanted to be bothered with; I just didn't have the energy or creativity. So, I opted not to go. I missed the opportunity to attend cosmology school because I was afraid of the unknown of going to another new school in the next new school year. Also, another student told me that I wouldn't fit in with the other cosmology students because of my weight. I was already self-conscious about my weight, therefore, I opted not to attend. I didn't try to go to college, either. I feared the process. I was extremely impressed with my sister. She enrolled into college without any assistance from me or my parents.

I found comfort in working a 9 to 5. I worked my first job at the age of 15. Yep, I've been working since I was 15 years old. I worked my first job without a break and at 17 years old, I started my job with the Federal Government. My goal was to work for Federal Government the rest of my life. I started at the very bottom of the pay scale. Thirty (30) years later I'm still working at the same agency. I was determined to do what I needed to do to reach my comfortable pay goal. I only sought positions in which I knew I could accomplish without facing challenges when I was younger. As my skills increased, I was more open to challenges. I have exceeded my expectation but, many times, I still felt like people didn't see me because of my weight. I felt like I was invisible to management because of my weight; regardless of the many contributions I made to the organization.

At 27, I had no kids. I transitioned to a new position with a potential to be promoted. I had my own apartment and car. I was moving into the comfort zone. My focus was making more money. Then, I realized that I need to be accomplish more in life. I decided to pursue my undergraduate degree and travel. I was feeling accomplished until I received the news that I was going to be a mommy. I told myself, "No!" No, I did not want children. Children made me uncomfortable and I had no intentions of being a single mother. How can I get out of this? I was miserable during my pregnancy. It was a very uncomfortable time in my life. It was nothing I could do to avoid this uncomfortable feeling, but to go home to my parents where I could feel a since of comfort. Eventually, I adjusted well to motherhood. The first four (4) years everything fell in place. I was managing well with the help from my family. The next 15 years of motherhood was the most challenging, especially because my child refused to move to my comfort zone. It was like he was holding on for dear life to avoid that zone. I couldn't understand why he had put me in all of these uncomfortable predicaments. Every one of his successes came with a challenge. I was always uncomfortable during the process. It took me twenty (20) years to understand that he is uncomfortable being comfortable and my girlfriend said that, "God had something bigger in store for his life and that is why his achievements didn't come easy", and he remains living outside of his comfort zone. I realized I was trying to push him in the comfort zone, so that I can return to my comfortable place.

Finally, I was in total comfort, I thought. I had a nice income, I loved my job in which I'm totally comfortable. I have two homes. My son is a college student with full scholarships and now, I can sit back and reap the benefits of the blessing from God. I was truly blessed, but I wasn't happy. I wasn't comfortable. I had no energy. I'm was almost three hundred (300) pounds again. Wait! I did what I was supposed to do. I thought, "Why am I not living my best life" like the folks on social media?

I began to watching people that I mentored in the work place doing big things and living their best life. That made me feel uncomfortable and resentful. I knew how to mask my jealousy and I didn't like feeling that way. I would see people travelling all over the world. I would think, "How are they doing that because I know how much money they make?" I would ask myself, "How do you live your best life?" However, I could not even articulate my WHY in life. Nothing excited me other than coming home sitting in my recliner, watching TV, having something good to eat and scrolling through social media watching what others were doing. I didn't even enjoy that routine.

New Years Eve of 2017, I decided I'm not making a resolution for 2018 because it was dumb, and I had no intentions of accomplishing anything, especially, losing weight. I'm over that. I felt like an old lady. I didn't feel comfortable going around people and believe it or not, I am, actually, a people's person. This was difficult for me, because my husband is full of energy and life. He lives his best life everyday, regardless of not having all the things I was told you must have to be comfortable. So, I was jealous of his energy and would not be so nice at times. I love him because he didn't let it bother him or stop him from living his life. He loves me unconditionally and he loved to feed me. He really thought that was what made me happy. In March 2018, my cousin was posting a product on social media that helps people lose weight make, and that would make people feel better and healthy. I told myself "I'm not even going to try anything in a box to lose weight!" I'm not taking a bunch of pills before each meal, wear a patch and drink a bunch of shakes. I been there done that. One day, she sent me a before and after picture of her and invited me to her product party. Even though, I was not thrilled about attending, I decided to go only to support her. The day before her party, I went to a birthday party for my friend's husband. Once again, I was in that mood of not wanting to be around people and especially a lot of people I didn't know. I committed and since, I am faithful, I had to go. I was so miserable, but and everything was so nice. I wanted to dance but, couldn't step outside my comfort zone to get out of the chair. My husband went with me. He always served as my comfort blanket at places where there were a lot of people and parties. His fun meter was off that night, so he was no help to me. On the way home, I keep replaying in my head how uncomfortable I was at this party. It was an unusual discomfort. Reflecting back on my past, I can now see God was trying tell me something.

The next day was my cousin's Wakaya Launch Party. While there, mentally, I tried to find the catch. When the gentleman began the presentation, I yelled out "I ain't selling nothing", he gathered himself and nicely said, "Ma'am there is no selling." Let's just say at the end of the presentation I wanted to buy whatever they were selling. After, leaving this party I was so excited and couldn't wait to start. I had not felt excitement like this in a long time. Wait! This is God again, how can a Network Marketing presentation bring out an excitement I had not experienced In a long time. Network Marketing is the last thing I want to do in my life.

Ever since leaving that Wakaya Launch Party, I have been confidently, kicking down the invisible comfort zone tape that has surrounded me for majority of my life. I never thought I needed personal development before now. I didn't like motivational speakers. I thought they talked too much and I have common sense. Now, I'm soaking up their wisdom. I've removed so many boundaries I set for myself and see the opportunities before me. I often think about all of the missed opportunities due to being afraid to step outside my comfort zone.

Not only am I living outside my comfort zone, I've lost eighty (80) pounds. And, this has help boost my confidence. I lived my entire life, mentally, seeing myself as I am now. There were days, I would look in the mirror and see the three hundred (300lb) Nicole, worried about what people would think and not feel accepted. I realized, it was just what I thought acceptance look liked to the world. I was that person who sat backed and watched others shine wishing I had the confidence to do what they were doing. Now, I'm living the life I played over and over in my head for years.

I'm approaching my 50th year of living and I'm just "Living my Best Life." I thought living your best life was travelling and doing extraordinary things. I discovered that it is just being self-aware, living your truth and not worry what others think. I'm writing this to say. "It's never too late." I have no regrets about waiting this long to live the life I'm living. At times, I still struggle with worrying about what others think. I'm still a work in progress. But, I finally recognize my Why. And, it is to help others **Live their Best Life** by sharing how to live a healthy physical and mental life. I recommend blocking out negative noise and let God lead you through your earthly journey.

Nicole Bowman-Smith Bio

Nicole Bowman-Smith is a former couch potato turned Boss. She was born in Washington, DC in 1970. She spent her elementary school years in New Jersey before moving back to the DMV area. She currently resides in Clinton, Maryland.

Nicole has spent all of her adult life working for the Federal Government. She has over 30 plus years of service. She is currently a Human Resources professional, specializing in federal pay and leave. She loves serving the men and women of her agency. She affectionally calls herself the Olivia Pope of the Human Resources Division.

Nicole is also an Independent Ambassador with Wakaya Perfection a health and wellness company since 2018. She discovered her inner Boss with the company by becoming a business owner, a product coach and a wellness advocate.

Nicole has been married to Charles Smith for 9 years and the mother of an adult son Marcus Bowman and two bonus adult children Cortni Salley and the other Charles Smith Jr. She has two bonus grand children Emerson and Ezra.

Chapter 3
Opening the Treasure Box

By Chihuana Hunter

"Create a place for God and He will meet you there every time."

Opening the Treasure Box

The first thing I would like to say is that I have been afraid to tell my story. I had to realize that the perception that people will have of me after I tell my story and in sharing my truth, is none of my business. So, here we go!

In order to know who you are, sometimes you must go back to your childhood and even your parent past to see what happened. My story begins with my mom when she was 14 years old. She was molested by her uncle and became pregnant but, never told her mom that her uncle molested her. She never broke the silence until about a year before her death; she told her older sister. When I was about 37, I called my aunt to ask her if she could set up a meeting for me to meet the man my mom was telling me who my father was. At that point, she told me who our (me and my brother) real father was my great uncle. She explained that my mom made her promise not to tell me until she was dead. So, my mom went to her grave not telling me who my father was. That code of silence was put on my mom, at 15 years old, when she gave birth to me & my twin brother. He was born with a mentally illness. My mom never told us what really happened. She said we were another man's children who never really claimed us.

After having us, she met my stepdad who was in the military. They started dating, got married and moved to Texas. We were babies. I don't remember much but I'll start where I remember. I remember us living in the projects in Dallas. There were good days and bad days. This one day, I remember my stepdad fighting my mom and hitting her with a bed slack. All I could hear was screaming and crying. My stepdad was a very jealous man. I was in my room crying, nervous and biting my nails. That has affected me for years. I still bite my nails when I get fearful or nervous, especially, if I don't have acrylic on my nails. This was my first encounter with domestic violent in the home.

I believe my mom married him to get away from Florida, because she was so young and didn't want to struggle with two kids by herself, especially, being so young. We moved from the projects to South Dallas and that's where it began for me. My stepdad used to use drugs. I didn't understand why he was filled with rage, but now I understand. We lived in these white apartments. I remember days when my stepdad fought my mom. The arguing and fighting seemed to happen all the time, so, my mom started to hang out with some of girlfriends frequently. She would leave me and my brother home with him. Often, she would stay out late. S would say she was going to the store and wouldn't come back for a long time or the next day. Of course, that led to more fighting. You never know why people do what they do. While my mother was out doing her thing with her friends, he started to do things to me. I was so young, I didn't know it was wrong. I was in elementary school. I never told my mom because they were already fighting, and I didn't want to be the cause of more fighting. Even worse, I felt she would not have believed me. So, I kept quiet. That code of silence seemed to have embedded itself in me at that point. I said nothing to no one.

My stepdad never had sexual intercourse with me. I thank God that he didn't. But, he would suck on my toes and do oral sex on me. As a little girl I didn't know what to do or say and my mom was not there to protect me either. Later, we moved to a gray and white house on that same street and at this point I was in the 3rd or 4th grade and they were still fighting. Then my mom started to use drugs and she started hanging out even more with her friends. So, of course the same things were happening to me. One instance he masturbated in front of me after doing what he did to me. I didn't know what to do or who to tell because I didn't know who would believe me. I found this to be the case with most children that is being abused; they keep silent and act like nothing has happen to them. From these experiences, you don't know it's wrong until you grow up and learn about these things. But, to make it to adulthood, you're at point when you " I made it out" but, you still don't tell nobody.

Finally, they broke up had after having a bad fight. He threw all my mom's stuff in the front yard and put us out. He fought her badly that day. The house was torn up. Me, my mom and my brother another set of apartments on that same street. I was in the 6th grade and my mom never knew what happen to me. She went to her grave not knowing. As a matter fact I never told anybody, except my husband. My mother, even though I believe she never want to, ended up being single anyway to raise me and my brother by herself.

My brother always needed special attention so when my mom and stepdad broke up, I had to grow up fast and help her with him. I had to learn to fix his food, give him medicine, protect him from hurting himself and change his diaper. My mom worked a lot to keep us somewhere to stay. We stayed on this same street until I was in the eleventh grade. When I was in the eighth grade I met my first boyfriend; whom I thought was the best boyfriend. All the girls wanted him because he was so cute. When I was in the 10th grade he started to fight me. This this bought back memory of what I had come out of with my mom. He was jealous just like my stepdad. But of course, I didn't tell anybody because I was afraid, because I had to go to school with him every day. One day he slapped me so hard at school in front of our lockers and my classmates. It was embarrassing. One night, he chased me in our apartments when I was coming from a party in the apartments. This was when I, finally, got tired of being abused. I hid behind cars trying to get to my apartment hoping to get in the house before he got there. I could hear him saying, "when I get you, I'm going to kick your ass." That freighting me so bad I knew then I had to leave him along. Again, I never told nobody what happened to me with that relationship, I was just glad to be out.

Then I was introduced to my ex-husband by my then, best friend. My ex-husband was 4 years my senior. He was nice and took care of me and my mom. He gave us whatever we needed. He had come from an amazing Christian family and his parents were the best in-laws I could ever ask for. I fell in love with them first and then him (I laugh about this, but it's true.) The only thing was, he was not as perfect as I thought. He had drinking problem; which at the time, I didn't think was a big deal because I was

32

young, and he was older. He had a great job and was not hitting on me or cursing me out. So, I stayed with him because I was getting ready to go off to college anyway. He would take care of me in school and help my mom. Since, I was away at school, I really didn't pay any attention to the drinking. I would come home some weekends from school to be with him. I ended up pregnant with our first son and then, we got married. I realized, I did the same thing my mom did; married an older man because I didn't want to raise my son by myself. Here I go in the same cycle as my mom, with a man that is an acholic. I felt like I didn't have a choice either, because my mom was moving back to Florida and she told me to stay here with him. I did and we had 2 more children and was married for 13 yrs.

When we were in our 1st year of marriage, he hit me, and I told him then if you ever hit me again that would be it. I didn't want to go thru what I had already being thru so many times in my childhood. In those 13 years I dealt with the drunkenness, staying out all night & the cheating. I would be up all-night crying. I had 3 small kids and was afraid to raise them by myself. I remember trying to find out his location because he would come home. I would call hospitals, jails and detox centers to see if he was there. Back then, we didn't have cell phones; we had beepers. He would never call me back. I was a nervous wreck all the time; arguing with him about the drinking and how I didn't want my kids to grow up and be drunks. To this day he still drinks, and it had been the cause of him losing a lot in his life. Well he did hit me again and after 12 years our marriage ended in divorce. After that, I moved into a 2-bedroom apartment with my 3 kids; I was in school and had 2 jobs. Then I met the man whom I am now married to. We met in down-town Dallas and dated for 3 years.

I remember seeing him every morning; until one day he said something to me. My husband says he knew I was his wife when he tried to break up with me and his ribs started to hurt. See he tried to pull that friend card, but still wanted boyfriend benefits. What he didn't realize is that I was not going to chase after him. I did not let him meet my kids until months before we got married. When he asked me to marry him, I told him I came as a package. He would come over on the weekends when the kids were home and gel with them. I had to do it that way because I was afraid to expose my kids to a stepdad. I would always, mentally, reflect to what happen to me as a stepchild. Not to say he would have done that, but it was just a phobia of mines that I had to get over. I have a daughter and it's no way I wanted her to experience what I did. My husband is a great man who has been there for all my kids. He has taken on the father role since the day we were married. He taught them all to drive. He constantly provided for them. Even to this day, if it is needed, he still provides for them. He has never, not one day, said those are not his kids. He has always wanted the best for them. He has been a great example for my kids as to what a man should be to his wife and his family. He has never disrespected them and has always taken care of us. The day we got married he said, "As long as you keep my haircut, feed me, and clothe me, then you can take the rest of the money for bills; you and the kids." Still to this day it's the same way. God really blessed me when he gave me him. With all I had been through, I didn't need another bad experience. Even after everything I had being threw, I had to trust because I knew I didn't want to be by myself for the rest of my life. I did not want my kids to grow up without a home with a foundation.

My husband came to the marriage without any kids because his daughter was killed in a car accident when she was a year and half by a drunk driver. So, when I was 36 years old we started a procedure to have my tubes untied. We wanted to a child together. After several pregnances that didn't go full term, we were finally successful with going through invitro. I was pregnant with twins at 39 and started to miscarry at 5 weeks of my pregnancy. But, a miracle happen; when one of the embryo stayed and I had a full term birth. God granted my husband the son he was praying for. We have now been married for 19 yrs. and it has been great to be married to a man of God who loves his wife and his children. We now have 3 grown kids who are doing very well for themselves. The oldest is an Account Executive for a major company. Our daughter is a mother to our two grandchildren and pursuing a Nursing degree. Then we have one who has graduated from college with his bachelor's degree and is a transfer graduate at another college pursuing a master's degree and his dream to go play professional football. I thank the Lord for all he has brought me through.

In the past and I have always wanted to be in a place to hear God's voice. In 2016 I heard the voice of the Lord. "He said you create me a place and I'll meet you there every time". I didn't understand, so of course, I had to go to God and say what do you mean? Well he reminded me of the movie War Room where the lady had a pray closet in her home. So, I said, "Oh ok want me to create a prayer closet?" So, I did and that is where I have been able to get over what happen to me in my past. All these years I suffered in silence with no one to tell or that I felt would believe me and understand. This book Breaking the Code of Silence, Now! is my way of helping somebody else who may be suffering in silence with no one to talk to or turn too. We can always turn to God, but we must be able to create a space for him where he can meet us at. If it's not in your closet in secret, let in be in your heart. He will not come in and help you with any hurt you may be experiencing until you open your heart and give Him the space where he can meet you at. The closet has been a haven where I go and cry out to the Lord. I take him all my hurts, fears and concerns and he meet me there every time. Thank you, Jesus

A lot of times aliments and sickness in our bodies can come from hurts, stress, guilt, pain, grudges, anger or unforgiveness we may be holding on to. A lot of times holding on to what happen to us causes us to eat, lash out at others, bad relationships and our lives to be in rolling ball effect of one thing after another. That's because you are not free and living in turmoil. I had a mini stroke the day before Mother's Day in May of 2018. It was due to high blood pressure, but again stress and other things can cause that to be elevated. That experience has changed my life forever, because I had to let go of a lot of pain from my past and now move forward in freedom. I was in the hospital for 4 days and then transferred to a rehabilitation home for 3 weeks where I had to learn to walk and talk all over again. During that time, I was not afraid of what God had in store for me but what I do know is that we go thru events in our lives to be an example and a witness to somebody else. God used me for many people to hear a word from him so if that what it took for me to relay a message to his people, then I'm ok with that. We must be grateful when God choose us to be a messenger for Him even when we are going through our situations.

I feel that when your past or your parent's past is in silence it's like it's a code that no one speaks of. You just know not to say something. But, it is really a stronghold on our lives and it does not allow nobody else to be helped by what you have been through. It's a trick of the enemy, because he doesn't want you to be free from bondage. He wants you to live with depression, guilt, and shame. I'm here to let you know that you don't have to live with depression, guilt, or shame. Tell your truth to help yourself and someone else who is struggling. It alright to say, that you were hurt by somebody. We hold ourselves back from speaking up and out because of the shame, fear of not been believed or a fear of being disowned by our friends and family. That was my case and I struggled with it all my life until I took it to God in prayer and He told me I can deliver you from all hurt, shame, guilt and depression. We can't worry about what no one will say or do, but we must trust God that he will deliver us from that stronghold. Somebody is waiting to hear your voice; until you speak up, the person that your voice is assign too will not be free. So, it's your time to speak up and be free and help somebody else become free.

Create that place in your heart for God to come in and meet you there and so he can help you Break The Code of Silence, Now! When that code of silent is broke, you start to open a treasure box with all kind of jewels and gems that are inside you. Until you break free those things that you want to be free to do will seem so far away or impossible to do to you, but with Jesus all things are possible. Open the box with your voice of freedom to be heard to be able to help yourself, friends, family and the souls that you are assigned too. No longer can you be hidden or held back from the true calling that God has on your life once you open the treasures that is stored in you. You are a treasure and the world need to experience all the valuables you have inside of you. It is for them to know that they have treasures that need to be opened. When I started to open my treasure box in my soul, I found out that I have a voice, talents, and gifts that has help me start a business. And that is a blessing to many. I found peace, joy and happiness in opening my treasure box because no longer am I held back from what I'm supposed to be doing and the people that need my help.

Chihauna Hunter Bio

Chihauna Hunter is married to Bobby Hunter and proudly celebrating 19 years of marriage. She is the mother of four: Carlton, De'Ashley, Marcus, and Bobby Jr. and she has 2 grandchildren's Ja'Miya and Ja Marion. Chihauna is a Lincoln High School alumnus and attended El Centro Community College where she received her Associate Applied Science Management degree. She is currently seeking her Bachelor of Science degree in Logistics Supply Chain Management at UNT-Dallas where she is a Senior. She worked for Bank of America for 20 yrs. and retired in 2011. She is also a member of Purity with Purpose, a 12-week discipleship course for women and was a fall 2007 graduate. Chihauna's spiritual gifts are exhortation and leadership. She loves to travel and especially to different Bed and Breakfast with her husband. She loves to read the word of God and her favorite scripture is Jeremiah 29:11 For I know the plans I have for you," declares the LORD, "plans to prosper you and not to harm you, plans to give you hope and a future". This scripture touches and speaks directly to her because God is letting her know that there is a plan for Chihauna's life and He knows what it is and that she must seek Him for that plan and He will prosper her and give her a hope for the future, no matter what the devil tries. As stated Chihauna lives, breaths and speaks GOD IS AWESOME AND MIGHTY in her life!

Breaking The Code of Silence, Now!

38

Chapter 4
My Beneficent P.O.P. (Privilege of Power)

By Danielle Fee Vaughn

"The KEY is to unlock dollars & differences by becoming the change"

My Beneficent P.O.P.
Privilege of Power

If you could only know a bit about me, I suppose the first thing I would tell you is that I was born in Houston, Texas. I like to tell people that's more than likely where they came up with that saying "Houston, we have a problem". My childhood was complicated, my parents were married and divorced twice to each other. My mom, in fact, was wife #2 & #5. Therefore, I have always said my dad loves my mom the most because he married her twice. I think before they had me, possibly, their lives were happy and filled with endless possibilities. I heard stories of how they used to have fun and even go to their neighbors for things like BBQ's with my older sister Danette. I would see pictures of them with my sister, but there were none of me. My dad worked all the time. Unfortunately, my dad repeated a generational cycle of physical & mental abuse. This wasn't a good combination for my young mom, she left 6 months pregnant with me due to an altercation, which I believe is what led to me being born with the left side of my brain damaged and my left leg shorter than my right.

I was brought into this world disabled and fighting for my life. Mom first noticed this at 4 months old because she would stand me on her lap my left leg would always give. She took me to an orthopedic specialist who diagnosed me disabled. The Dr. explained I would always walk with a limp and my motor skills would be off. Mom and grandma kept working my legs for 6 months. Grandma kept praying. She told my mom "when you take her back, she is going be ok". When returning to the doctor, everyone, including the doctor, were amazed to find out that my legs were now equal. It was said to be a miracle! That news was great but, the onward battle of custody, support, and responsibilities of my sister and I never ended.

Of course, during the single parenting moments of life my mother did have to go to work. I remember one day specifically when I was an eight-year-old innocent little girl. It was my birthday. Everybody was having a good time. I went to get some Kool-Aid. Then, an older male cousin poured the Kool-Aid for me and smiled and led me upstairs to "play a game". It was a cool looking foosball table. I walked over to it and looked over at him to wait for him so that we could begin. I watched him as he walked past the foosball table straight to the door. I watched him lock it. He turned around and had an evil look in his eyes that I will never ever forget. I was molested. I can still smell the sweat of him from time to time. I still suffer sleepless nights. I still can't be near a room with a foosball table without anxiety or breaking out in tears. He threatened that if I told anyone he would kill my parents, so I waited till I was 24 and married and assured by my husband that it was safe to tell my parents, so I did.

I attended that family function that year with my new husband and told my parents and yes, my mom says looking back she knew something had happened; she just didn't know what exactly or who because when she asked, I said nothing. All she knew was I started acting out. Fighting all the time. Wetting the bed, my behavior spun out of control, I slapped my step dad across the face at our dinner table, kicking animals, biting other kids, angry all the time, afraid to be in a room alone, real clingy, and up until that point I was allegedly a good child. I refused to leave my dad's side. I never wanted to go without him to the point where she thought he might have done something. I personally just knew my dad was my protector and if anybody was going to try anything else, they were going to have to go through him and that was not going to be an easy task. He was strong, educated and great at his working jobs. He got promoted often.

Between the moves and the ladies, I got lost in the shuffle. I might add, he has the worse pick in so called step moms, too. My sister and I have nicknames for them all. None which are positive. One of my step moms, I knocked out with a Q-ball. My sister was always good at braiding. One step mom tried to force Danette to braid Her daughter's hair when she didn't feel good and I said "Nope, not today" she told me to "shut up". I said "NOPE". She went to call dad and I yanked it right out the wall. Yes! That's right. She went to hit me; I ran downstairs laughing. She came down those stairs screaming "why you little winch" she chased me four times around our dining room table then I darted into our pool table room and when she approached, I nailed her so hard with that Q-ball it knocked her unconscious. I ran to the garage phone and called mom because I thought I killed her. My mom came racing over but, she lived further away so my dad got home first. Yikes! You guessed it. I was knee deep in trouble. My step mom lied through her teeth about what had happened. I got in so much trouble and the beaten I took for what I did and did not do was unforgettable. Shortly, after this incident, my step mom was killed by a young drunk driver. I wished I could say I felt sorry about this but, I felt this was GOD protecting me from further harm.

Quickly, I gained another step mom, she was wealthy, I was bought with gifts, money and things yet, love was still absent. I was put into so many extra activities to keep me away from home and her. It was quite genius. She got my dad all to herself. Honestly, I wanted to be with my own mother but, my 8-year-old sexual abused traumatic experience felt safer with my dad even though I was physically abused by him. The experience of what had happened blinded my ability to make that decision for myself. I was just existing.

Finally, mentally drained by his relationship, my dad, begged my mother to take him and me back in when I was 14years old. She did for love. They re-married Christmas eve that year. We were a happy family. Only to learn a few months later on valentine's day, at my girlfriend's house, I overheard her mom and her friend discussing a man that fit my dads' cars personalized licenses plate description that I decided to walk on into the living room and listen to their conversation. I was intrigued to hear this woman talk about this necklace & pants she had on he had bought. I continued to listen as she talked about how funny it was that his wife which she referred to as "His B****h" and her kids didn't know that he was spending his money on her and her five children and how she was driving his yellow Cadillac with those personalized plates around our town. At this point, I had heard enough. I got up! I smiled! I walked towards my girlfriend's front door, I looked over and said "Hey, is that your car out here? your doors open" she got up. I politely held that door open for her, and as she passed through it, BOOM! My fist hit her so hard in the back of her skull she went like humpty dumpty right on down those 7 front porch steps. I jump down right along with her like spider man and I drug that heifer by her long brown hair to that huge tree in the front yard and bashed her head in it all the while yelling at her "I'm the B****Hs daughter and this belongs to me" and I took that necklace right off her throat. I then said, "oh this belongs the B****h too" and took them pants right on up off her. Next thing I know my grandma was pulling me off this bleeding lady screaming "enough already" because I refused to let go. I was trying to end her life. My grandma forced me, that necklace, those pants, and my rage all in her car, and we went home. She made me call my mom at work against my will. I called her and told what I had done. My mom calmly said to me "Don't worry about it, I will handle it when I get home". She did. I waited with anticipation. I was so freaking nervous. My dad came home first and was hotter than the fourth of July fireworks display. He blamed me. He ultimately told my mom because they were fighting so much, he was "keeping his options open".

Well, for me, I held so much guilt. My sister admitted she hated me for many years because of this. She felt if I would have remained silent, I could have kept our family together and she would have had a father in her life; which she has wanted and struggled with all her life. I told her for me I was screwed either way. If I remained silent, I was lying to mom. If I told I was telling on dad. I was put in a no-win situation. I had to make an adult life altering decision at 15 which was unfair for me. I have had to deal with much depression because of this. Although, I was at fault I knew at 15 right from wrong. I based my decision at 15 on doing what He always said to do and then he was upset that I did the right thing. The right thing for me is to always tell the truth even if it hurts. Often it does. Due to these circumstances, my parents divorced again, and he married again instantly. Nope, I am not kidding! The circus started up again with a new ring leader; too bad it wasn't it him this time.

All my life, I looked up to my dad for being such a firm, educated leader. This time was different. He failed at his championship race lap. I picked up the mantel and had to face my worse fears, rejection and abandonment. It caused me many tears and sleepless nights. I think through all the women, marriages and loss of my mother's love on multiple occasions, he lost his luster for unconditional love and happiness. I had to find the strength to for-give him and, the little girl inside me who just wanted to be loved. I've learned that in order to free myself and stand in my privilege of power, I had to set boarders around my frame (my body, my heart, mind, soul). Just Like a picture frame all photos don't fit. Neither do all families. I had to stop try-ing to make a family that didn't exist. When I finally accepted that I had to be Loyal 2 ME, I started, originally, to struggle to define normalcy and what real love looks and feels like. The only love that I am certain of is the love that I have for my own children. So, reflecting upon things that have hap-pened to me in my life, I have a clear understanding at how and why I have made the poor choices of toxic relationships that did not serve me well. It took a long time to regain love, dignity and self-worth.

I continue to work on that self-love regimen daily. I started out slowly by writing on my bathroom mirror notes to myself as to why I did not hate myself and why I was worth love. I wrote sayings on bright colored post-it-notes that read, "You're the best kept secret." I would put them in my purse, inside my checkbook, on my visor in my car. Then, I graduated to healthier eating and exercise choices. I began to finally smile and have fun again. I felt lighter and started to feel in some control of my own life. The stronger I became the more negativity I removed with ease. Having to "unpack my past" and deal with the choices I've made, required much faith. Now, I not only take time to make better choices for both me and my chil-dren, I share my experiences to help others who are struggling with similar circumstances. I want to give self-confidence to women that feel that they can't get up from the place of despair. I need them to get off the floor and ROAR! I now stand in my Beneficent Privilege of Power!

Danielle Fee Vaughn Bio

As a Certified John Maxwell Speaker Trainer, Certified Parent Educator, Special Education Advocate, Life coach, Interpreter for the deaf, and a single mother to three children with multiple disabilities, Dani is passionate about helping other single mothers and uses her expertise to successfully teach how to gracefully live with the daily challenges of parenting special needs children.

She is the founder of The Dani Keys Organization that provides resources, support, & enrichment services for single moms. Additionally, she is the founder of The Fierce Girl Company & Keys 4 Needs, a non-profit organization that provides opportunities for these mothers children, friends, and family members to be able to help support them in creative ways.

Breaking The Code of Silence, Now!

Chapter 5

It Was Already Purposed

By DeShanta Hinton

"Remember in this life you are going to have to live with all the decisions you make so be sure that you are comfortable with those decisions and are accepting of the consequences that come from those decisions. It is your life and you only get one...this is the show...the stage is set...Ready, Set, Action. Make your life count!"

It Was Already Purposed

Life is full of choices, good choices, bad choices, and choices that you make because you just are not sure about what else to do in life. From the time I was in elementary school I knew that I wanted to be a lawyer. That desire to be a lawyer can really be attributed to the fact that my father was incarcerated, and I deeply loved him. My parents were high school sweethearts in the early seventies when I was born. My mother, Barbara was a petite woman with a lot of attitude and my father, Gregory was a suave man with a lot of street smarts. The seventies were a time when music had meaning, neighbors would correct your kids, and communities were like families. My mother was one of eight children and my father was one of five, so I suppose that coming from those big families is why they decided I would be one of one!

When I talk about my childhood I always start by saying that I thank God that I was able to be a child and enjoy my childhood. I grew up not having to take on any adult responsibilities like some of my friends. During my childhood, my father spent a majority of the time incarcerated, so I was raised by my mother with a lot of influence from my maternal grandparents, Lizzie Mae & Howard because we lived with them. I thoroughly enjoyed living with my grandparents because everyone would gather at our house. On Saturday mornings I would get up to write the grocery list for my grandfather so that he could go to the store with my uncles. My family has always been close and as I reflect on my childhood it is funny to think that all four of my uncles would take my grandfather to the store. That's a clear example of the closeness of my family. During the holidays all of the family would gather at my grandparent's house, where we would listen to music, dance, and just enjoy quality family time together.

I have spoken a lot about my maternal grandparents because they impacted my life in a very special way; however, I would be dismayed if I did not mention my paternal grandmother, Jabella. You see she was the main reason my father and I had such a close relationship. It was my grandmother that would put her Lincoln Town car on the road to take those four hour drives to and from Pennsylvania so that I could visit my father in those federal penitentiaries. At times these trips would consist of other family members or even friends of my father but mostly it was just the two of us traveling the road listening to Phoebe Snow on the radio. My grandmother would drive through those winding mountains during the spring and summer when the sun would be shining in the sky, as well as, the fall when the trees would be changing colors looking like a box of crayons and in the winter when the snow would cover the mountains. These trips meant so much to me and each time I was overjoyed to see my father.

When we would take these road trips I would always be eager to get on the road because I knew that meant I would be that much closer to spending time with my father. I would try to be good company for my grandmother and stay awake; however, it never failed that I just couldn't stay awoke for the whole trip. We would often stop for breakfast at Perkins restaurant which as about thirty minutes before you got to the penitentiary. Imagine this older black lady with her young granddaughter entering this predominantly white town of Lewisburg, PA so it was interesting seeing how the attitudes of the people changed over the years because we visited this restaurant during the seventies, eighties, and nineties.

These visits were a little scary knowing that my father was here made it all better for me. The penitentiary looked like an old castle with walls so high you could not see over them and towers all around with guards watching your every move from the car to the gate. We would park the car and begin our journey to the gate to be welcomed into the Lewisburg Federal Penitentiary. Once inside you would have to complete the visitor form, provide your identification, and remove all metal before going through the metal detector. After being cleared by the guards, we were escorted to the visiting hall. Upon entrance we would take our form to the front desk and wait for the guard to assign us a seating section. We would go to our assigned section and wait for my father to enter the visiting hall. The visiting hall was a big open area with about four rows of two chairs connected to a table from the beginning of the room until the end of the room. On the side of the visiting area there were vending machines and a television area. My father loved egg salad sandwiches, so I would always get one so that it would be waiting for him when he came into the visiting hall. Whenever my father entered the visiting area he would great everyone that was there and save the best for last which was me! He would pick me up and give me the biggest hug and kiss; however, as I got older picking me up was not happening anymore but we stuck with the hug and kiss forever.

During these visits we would talk about everything from the things in the letters to what hadn't been mentioned in the letters. Sitting in the visiting area was like sitting at home in the living room because even though there were other families visiting and it was loud because children would be playing in the television area when my father and I would talk it would be like we were the only people in the room. Not that my father would neglect the other people that had come to visit him, but he would make certain to spend quality time with me. The visits would be over at 3pm so when it would get close to time to leave I would get a little sad and my father would use this time to tell me how much he loved me and how proud he was of me which would make me smile. I would always be the last one he touched whether it was in the greeting or saying goodbye which always made me feel extra special.

Growing up I spent a lot of my time at Grandma Jabella's house because the street was always full of fun and people were always outside and not to mention it was easier for us to travel being already together. When I look back over my life I know that God had his hand on my life even when I was not acknowledging Him. The Bible says, "That his grace is sufficient" and "His mercies are new to us each day." The place where my grandmother lived and where I loved to spend my time was known as one of the most notorious open-air drug markets in Washington, D.C. called Hanover Place. Hanover Place was not only an open-air drug market but a street where neighbors were family and family meant everything. I think I liked being around Hanover so much because in a subtle way my family and friends of the family felt empathy towards me because my father was incarcerated; therefore, they would show me favoritism in their own way. Of course, you know what they say, "favor isn't fair" but I will walk in mine because what God has for you is for you!

Almost every summer my Uncle Alvin would host a bus trip to either Florida or Myrtle Beach and you know that trips costs no matter where you are going; however, I don't remember my mother ever paying for me to go on these trips nor did she provide me with any spending money. At the beginning of every school year, my Uncle Boo would come to my house with at least two big black construction trash bags of brand-new clothes for me. Although my father's siblings may have been upset with him for returning to prison, they still loved him, and this was their way of showing their love for him by extending it to me. Looking back during this time I don't recall my uncles ever saying "I love you" a lot but their actions spoke louder than any words that weren't ever spoken.

I can often remember thinking why did my father have to be incarcerated? Was he really a bad guy? It was during these years of my life that I started thinking about becoming a lawyer so that I could help my father come home. It was also during these years that my father and I started developing a relationship with each other through phone calls and letters. I begin just writing one-page letters; however, as I got older and life got more challenging the letters started being longer. I also wanted to make sure that my father didn't miss any important moments, so I would make the letters as descriptive as possible. I would end each letter with "Always Smiling" which meant that no matter the circumstances good or bad that I would always be smiling, and I wanted him to be doing the same. The phrase just came so easy to me whenever I would post pictures on social media platforms like Instagram or Facebook; however, I didn't even realize where the phrase came from until I was going through some old letters and saw it. While my father would write me letters, one special thing he would do is have someone in the prison make me a really nice birthday card and then it seems like everyone in the prison would sign the card. I couldn't wait for my birthday because I knew if I didn't get anything I would be getting mail that would make my smile light up like a Christmas tree. Another special memory is that my father would send me money for my birthday because he worked in the prison (he wasn't paid much at all) but he would make sure to send me a birthday gift. Although it was not a lot of money, for me it really was the thought that counted, and I appreciated it so much because I know how little he had for himself.

Anyone that knows me, or my father knows that I am a "Daddy's girl" from the heart. My father was the first man that I loved and there is nothing like a daddy-daughter bond. With that being said I never felt any type of way about going to prison to visit my father or people knowing that my father was incarcerated. What I mean by that is I wasn't happy that he was incarcerated but I wasn't ashamed or embarrassed either. I actually used my father's imprisonment as my motivation to become a lawyer as I have stated over and over again! He is also the reason I am so selective in the people that I have in my inner circle.

Growing up without a father's physical presence is hard I am not going to lie and make it seem like everything was a piece of cake. I do believe that watching the choices of my parents especially my father made me think differently about things in life. When I would see my friends with their dads it would make me a little sad about my situation. Although we talked a lot on the phone and through letters, there is nothing that could take the place of my dad being present physically in my life. My life could have gone down a very different path; however, God didn't see fit for it to be that way. Jeremiah 29:11 says, "For I know the thoughts that I think toward you, saith Jehovah, thoughts of peace, and not of evil, to give you hope in your latter end." It's not like my path was clear and easy by no means; there were bumps and bruises along the way. It's just that I made up in my mind a very long time ago that I was going to be successful in life no matter what I was doing in life. I don't even think my father really know the impact he had on my life just by being incarcerated. As I transitioned from a young child to a teenager I began to look at life differently because people began to show me who they really were and what role they were playing in my life. There was one particular time that I can remember when my father was home and he was dating this lady that I didn't really like because I felt that she was taking him from me. At one point I stopped communicating with my father because I didn't want to be around him or her. This was a really tough time for me because I couldn't understand after all the time we had already lost why he wouldn't be trying to take advantage of the time that we have now. During this time, I was very angry with my father and that made me rebellious towards my mother, this was displaced anger I know now. I started as the old folks would say "smelling myself: meaning I was thinking I was grown, and I could make my own decisions about things in my life but my mother quickly gave me a reality check on got me back on the right track. From that day forward, I decided that I was going to have a positive impact on my own life, as well as, on the lives of those around me because being negative, sad, and rebellious were not attributes that I wanted attached to who I was in life.

So, I make it through my teenage years and enter young adulthood. At 20 years old I gave birth to my only child a bouncing baby boy named Dominique. During this time my father was incarcerated at USP Allenwood and so just like that my son's relationship with his grandfather began through visits and phone calls just like my childhood. I know that many people feel like they would never take their children to a prison and I respect those opinions; however, that was never my opinion and it probably had a lot to do with the way that I was raised. When parents aren't in the lives of their children, you have no idea what type of affect that will have on the child. I had many friends whose fathers were in the same city as them but still were not a part of their life. Even though my father was miles away he impacted my life the best way that he could give the limitations because of his situation.

Now that I was a parent it was very clear to me that all my future decisions would be based on the best interest for myself and my son. This became ever so clear especially when my son's father was murdered when he was nine months old. During this time, I had a lot of questions for God; however, at the end of the day I had to trust God knowing that He would not put more on me than I could bear. My favorite scripture which is Proverbs 3:5-6 says, "Trust in Jehovah with all thy heart, and lean not upon thin own understanding; In all thy ways acknowledge him, and he will direct thy paths" resonated with my spirit so strongly that I couldn't deny God was working in my life. God already knew that this situation would happen, and He knew that I could bear this trial. At this time like no other I had to trust God because he knew the beginning from end. He had already ordained that I would bring forth my son and raise him without a father. God knows what you need, and he prepares you for things in your life even when you don't know that you are being prepared. Since I grew up without my father I was able to help my son deal with his father being gone by getting involved in church and expressing to him that even though his physical father was not there, his heavenly father would always be there for him in life. It is somewhat ironic that I was raised without a father and now I would be doing the same thing with my son. Nevertheless, raising a black man as a single parent when there were some many things trying to go against God's plan...my testimony is that my son graduated High School, has NEVER been in incarcerated, and has a job as s DC Firefighter. All I can say is to God be the Glory because the prayers of the righteous avail much!

While I was raising my son, I started pursuing my Associates decree in Criminal Justice at Montgomery College. I would work all day and go to school at night while my mother would care for Dominique. This pattern continued as I pursued my Bachelor's degree in Criminal Justice, as well as, my Master's degree with a concentration in Human Resources and my Master of Business Administration at the University of Maryland University College. These were long days and longer nights because not only was I attending class in the evening, but I had to study too. And, of course, nothing was more important to me than coming home and spending time with my son before he went to bed each night. I never wanted to him to feel like I was busy doing all these things that came before him, no matter what I wanted him to know that he was first priority in my life and everything else was because of him and to benefit him in the future. My father was the inspiration for me starting college; however, I was the inspiration for me finishing college! In 2000, my father would get arrested on an armed robbery charge and receive life without parole because he was a third time offender. I think this is when I accepted the fact that my father was a career criminal. I certainly do not condone the behavior my father displayed that got him arrested; however, I understand that he thought he was doing what was best for him at the time. My father was a guy that would help his family and friends no matter what the cost.

Also during this time, I began to be more involved in my church as the church administrator, as well as, an intercessory prayer warrior. As an intercessor, you really have to be able to communicate with God because you are praying on the behalf of others and nothing is more intimate than prayer time with God. The more I would pray, the more God would reveal things to me which made me trust him the more. Of course, like all black families my grandmother took me to church when I was younger; however, as a teenager/young adult I stopped attending church. It wasn't until I had my son that I really started thinking that I need to get back in church because I'm going to need more than my own strength to raise my son, pursue a higher education, and just improve my life in every aspect. Strengthening my relationship with God was the best thing that has ever happened to me. God's love helped me through some dark times and allowed me to become more self-confident and share my gifts with others. God blessed me with the gift of intercession, as well as, the gift of being an encourager. When you know what your gifts from God are. You can walk around and not be intimidated by the enemy but be ready to establish your ground when the enemy begins to rear his head. Knowing whose you are and who you are gives you a boldness that can't be denied.

New Year's Day will never be the same for me in life. On the first Sunday of 2012, I received a call from my grandma Jabella that my father had committed suicide. After I got off the phone I sat on the bed and the tears just began to roll down my face. As I sat there I remember thinking yesterday before going to church service that someone was not going to make it into the New Year, never once thinking that it would be someone close to me. I got myself together and went to church just to be in the atmosphere of the intercessory prayer that would be going forth before the service that morning. I also wanted to let my church family know what was going on and get prayer for myself because I knew that this would be a heavy burden to bear for me. After I left church I went straight to my grandmother's house where all of the family and friends were gathering to remember my father. I will never forget that moment that I walked into the house and spoke to everyone and then went in the living room and lay on the couch and cried my little heart out. Nobody bothered me or came to check on me, they just let me have my moment to grieve for my father. As we prepared for my father's home going celebration I interacted with many of his friends and heard stories about how my father was such a good guy. Losing my father was a huge loss for me because even though he was incarcerated I never thought about my life without him being here.

God has always had his hand on my life even when I didn't recognize that He was covering me. I can truly say that all of my accomplishments can be attributed to God moving in my life not because of any goodness of my own but because of my faith that tapped into His grace, mercy, and favor that He saw fit to extend towards me. This life that you have is not your own, but it belongs to God, so it would be in your best interest to honor God with your life so that you can see your blessings manifest on this earth.

DeShanta Hinton Bio

DeShanta Nicole Hinton is a native Washingtonian. She is a mother, prayer warrior and a first time author. She was educated in the District of Columbia School System. She enjoys traveling, spending time with her family, and exercising. She grew up as a child of an incarcerated parent; therefore, she knows and understands firsthand the affect the criminal justice system can have on a family structure. Her upbringing motivated her to complete an Associate and Bachelor of Science in Criminal Justice, as well as a Master of Science in Human Resources and a Master of Business Administration.

DeShanta N. Hinton is employed as the Chief of the Human Capital Services Division of the U.S. Agency for International Development. She has over 28 years working in the federal government. DeShanta has served as a mentor for the Department of State Program and USAID where she mentored federal employees for career development. She has mentored women with the DC Project Connect. She served as a mentor for Streetwise Partners, were she won the Mentor/Mentee of the Cycle award.

Chapter 6

Why I Live and Love Differently

By Lisa A. Matthews

"We all have the gift to be resilient and shift the paradigm in how we choose to let pain define us."

Why I Live and Love Differently

"Don't call me dad" he said. These four words represent my very first memory of rejection. As an eight-year old, I remember being loss for words to ask, "why not?". I simply recall feeling confused, shocked, and humiliated. You see, earlier that day, my mom had just told me to get dressed because "my father" was on his way to pick me up. Thinking back to that day, I relished with excitement in the idea to spend time with him. For me, in every sense, he had done what most fathers would do to care for a child other than reside in the same home and I had decided that I would honor that by calling him "dad". That moment is so clear in my mind decades later with the memory of his piercing eyes staring and daring me to never acknowledge him by calling him "dad" again. So, I never did. This was the first time I can recall someone breaking my heart.

Staying in a child's place, I learned very fast that in order to maintain a relationship with him it had to be on his terms. In and out of my life for more than three decades, I respectfully followed rule number one which was to call him by his name. As I reminisce over the years I had with him, what I remember and appreciate most was the financial support and teachable moments that enabled me to achieve academically. As I became a young woman, there were heartfelt conversations and debates we shared about life and how he felt I should live it. When I think about the totality of the relationship, I realize that he never told me he loved me, never gave me a hug, and the obvious most hurtful feeling, he never acknowledged that I was his daughter. I did not understand until writing my story how this man's denial of me has had such a profound impact in how I lived and loved differently throughout my entire life. I see know how the underlying decisions I made in life were aligned to what I felt would make him accept me as his. Now after his death, I am left to unravel the mystery of the man who did for me as a father should yet love me differently. And I now am ready for the answer to my question as a child, "why not"?

Many who know me, will tell you that I am extremely analytical and a sleuth at best who will eventually find out what I need to know. The puzzle I desperately sought to solve surrounding the muted the story about "my father" and the shady presence he had in my life. There was this hidden code right before my eyes between my mother and the man I placed on a pedestal who at times was physically present in my life but detached in every emotional way a parent should not be. What I found out was a story of a tumultuous relationship between the two and while their time together lasted only a few years, a code of silence was made to hide a horrific incident where exposure would be detrimental to many lives forever.

It would take the untimely death of "my father" two years ago to give my mother reassurance and freedom to break the code and tell me that she lived in fear of this man all her life. What I learned was that while pregnant, my mother suffered emotional and physical abuse at the hands of "my father" before I even took my first breath. While this is her narrative to the story behind the story, incidents of their past have been corroborated by others for me to accept several parts of her story to be true. What I know now is this code of silence for my mother had more to do with her shame about the years of abuse she suffered at his hands coupled with his guilt about a near death incident that could have destroyed my mere existence. This secret and everything afterwards became the precursor to how I live and love differently.

Sadly, I learned after his death through confirmation of a DNA test that "my father" was my father. The realization before me is that I had my father in my life but was unable to connect with him as such because of the code of silence. The shame and guilt my parents lived with held them hostage thereby forged a denial for me to establish relationships with the other side of my family. I feel I lived a partial life half full. Accepting all of this has immersed me in my own guilt and shame behind the fact that my father, one of the greatest influences in my life was also the same man that attempted to destroy my existence.

Now knowing the history behind my parent's relationship, I understand now how I live differently by becoming "the fixer" for family and friends. I was on a hunt unbeknownst to me to be acknowledged, accepted and loved to compensate for what was denied to me by my father. My ability to be of help became my obsession that has now turned into a knack to advocate for others. Because my voice was loss as that eight-year-old girl, I now am the voice for the voiceless who are unable to solve problems that will help them afford basic needs they deserve. I recall a story of a dear friend who was wheelchair bound and could not get to her medical appointments because of a hiccup with a company's transportation system. She feared losing her job and receiving her dialysis treatment. Hearing her story tugged at my heart and within 30 minutes I wrote a letter that resolved this problem and the following day services were restored.

I love differently. I mask my hurt through a façade that my strength is greater than my pain. As a result, I feel that I am unable to love freely. Writing this chapter has caused me to face a realization that I am not over my first heartbreak. As a result, I compartmentalize relationships to avoid being hurt. As I process how the history behind my story is so relevant to the woman I am today, I now understand how not knowing why I was loved differently by my father held me hostage. I now realize that my defense mechanism to never hurt that way again was to build a wall brick by brick around my heart over the course of my life.

Building that wall gave has given me a false sense of security that I was okay. Unfortunately, it has created dynamics of many broken relationships with family and friends. I feel that I could not reciprocate their love to me because I question their intentions. I have been told that at times I lack empathy of the needs of others. I agree especially when it requires me to open my heart. I can recall many times being to self-absorbed in assuming people want more of me rather than to love with my heart. What I now acknowledge is that how I chose to live, and love created an afflicted internal battle indicative of being broken by my father.

As a woman writing in her truth, I leave you with the most powerful lesson I know. In order to gain clarity over the unknown, we must ask the tough questions even if we fear the answers in order to break the cycle. I acknowledge that my parents have their experience and I cannot allow their pain to be my pain. While I empathize with the longsuffering they endured in this code of silence, I feel that by sharing my story I am no longer held captive and I can freely begin to heal because I choose this platform to find my voice. I hope that if you are being held hostage to secrets you find a way to break the code of silence.

I mourn the loss of my father and it saddens me that it took nearly five decades to know the truth. I truly feel empowered unleashing this story and I smile as I think about God's timing. I am now living to love differently than before. Writing this story has released a rawness I typically would never share yet it has stretched me to be open and to accept and embrace my story as part of my testimony. What I learned most about this code of silence is that because I was loved differently, I determined my future through the lens of my past. If I knew then what I know now, I would have been more receptive to love through the pain with my heart rather than forecast a hurt that may not have existed or was not intentional. I now realize that as I work to heal from what I would define as one of the darkest periods in my life, God has made a way to shine the light to allow me to grow and use my story to uplift others.

While I continue to accept what I can never change as part of my story and experience, I end this chapter by telling you how I begin to move forward. I first had to acknowledge that as painful as it was to learn that my father made attempts to harm my mother to terminate her pregnancy with me – God had the final say and I truly know I survived for a reason. It matters to me to make that dash between the day I was born and the day I die count. I attempt to live with purpose in all that I do now and even more so as nearly five decades of this code of silence has had an impact on my life. I lived in the past of what was my experience as learned behavior where rejection, abandonment and denial of truth where my guide.

Today, I continue to work on focusing on the present. In quiet times the past illuminate in my place and space of peace where I recall the hurt and I spend wasted time and energy pointing fingers to place blame. I know that this only creates a victim mindset and I have done that for too long now. Pain does not disappear on its own – I realize that I must do the work. I am work in progress and as I try to forgive what I did not know, the reward in forgiving is more for me than for my parents. The experience and relationship of my parents is part of their story and I cannot continue to allow it to infuse my spirit. Forgiveness embodies self-love.

> *"Forgiveness is about empowering yourself, rather than*
> *empowering your past."*
> *-T. D. Jakes-*

Since my father's death, I find writing as one of the most freeing activities to which I can express my feelings. Journaling my thoughts give me the therapeutic space to be my most vulnerable, honest and authentic self. I have grown through this experience and well on my way to becoming a better me. The most important thing I had to do was to forgive myself in how I lived and loved differently and more importantly, to forgive myself for anyone I may have hurt along the way. Learning to let go and forgive has given me the power to hit the reset button to renew relationships of the past and the freedom to know that it's okay to let go of other relationships.

Finally, I leave you with this thought. Pain is inevitable. We know it will happen, yet in that moment of what pains us, we feel there is absolutely nothing we can do about it. Or can we? We all have the gift to be resilient and shift the paradigm in how we choose to let pain define us. To remain silent, we give consent for others to control how we live and love, barricading our feelings behind emotions of hurt, fear, anger and shame. Saying that we are broken, not realizing we had the power to fix it all along. We must disrupt this behavior and give ourselves permission to control the narrative of our lives and let power radiate over pain in order to live and love freely, happily and differently than before. - Break the code of silence in your life, now!

Lisa A. Matthews Bio

Lisa Matthews is a native Washingtonian. She currently for a national non-profit organization where her personal passion is aligned with its mission to strengthen communities. For over 15 years, she has been an agent for change and has served as a volunteer with numerous organizations where her intention is to empower individuals with disabilities and their families, and all who feel powerless to navigate systems that offer better outcomes that will improve the quality of their lives. Lisa is an Honoree Listee in the *2018 Who's Who in America* and has received several certificates of appreciation for her commitment to service. She is a co-author of the #1 International Bestseller book titled *The Sisterhood folios, Unbreakable Spirt*. Lisa has written articles for online publications and enjoys writing poetry. She also enjoys spending time with her family and friends.

Chapter 7

When I Decided Enough Was Enough

By Melinda Chervil Cobb

"Live life as happy as you can"

When I Decided Enough Was Enough

Friday March 19, 2019 at 3:19am I decided that today was enough! I realized I have been mentally, sexually and physically abused by many people. Yeah, that's sad. But very much true.

I am an African American woman born and raised in Chicago on the far south side. I was raised by two loving parents, in a two-parent household; which they were about 18-19 years young and doing the best that can to protect me from the everyday, bad reality. They made sure I wasn't around people that they felt was not living a life of destruction. My mom was over-protective from what I saw. She tried very hard to shield me from the wild-wild 100 (a neighborhood on the southside of Chicago.) Five years after I was born, they got married and then had my little sister, whom I admire and love so dearly.

Growing up as a little dark skinned-girl wasn't easy in the 80's. People were just getting out of the concept of not being beautiful if you were darker than the brown paper bag. If anyone knows about the paper bag method, they'll kind-of know what was taken place around this time. I used to think that people couldn't see me that I was too dark, and I was walking on the earth invisible. It was truly all in my head. My parents, grandparents and aunt and uncles loved me and admired how beautiful I was inside and out. But, when it came to me appreciating my dark skin, I didn't do that so well. I didn't realize how pretty I was, especial with all this beautiful melanin running through my veins. I was about 14 years old when I started loving me and my beautiful dark skin. This may seem pitiful and sad but, it's what I live through.

66

Now, what changed the way that I saw myself was an African Culture program called Upward Bound. This program changed my understanding. This program taught me about Black Is Beautiful. How to Love yourself and how to recognize self-hate. Then showed me how to love who you are and why you are as precious as gold and silver. Which I know now, and this story that I will tell you will open young dark girls' and boys' eyes to recognize how to avoid the signs of abuse. How I realized I was abused was shocking to me. It was hard to understand who I was and where I've been, until now!

The day was so dark and gloomy to me when I was asked to talk about my past. When I was asked to break the code of silence. My sister asked me to write this because I had a unique life experience. I said to my sister, "I don't have no code and I'm not silence. I am an out spoken person. I don't have any shame of who I am and where I been. I say what on my mind and tell any and ever one with no reservations, how I feel." However, this is how my story came about.

I really didn't know how to start and what I was going to write about. I sat down thinking about different things. like should this be about "My Father Cheating on My Mom for 43 years?" Should I write about my "Fathers Sickness and How it Hurt Me? Should I write about "How My Mom Makes Me Feel When I'm In Her Presence?" Should it be about "The Control That My Mom Had Over Me". Should it be about "The Sexual Assault I Endured When I Was 16"; when I walked out my front door to go see a friend of a friend that I didn't even know? Or, should I write about The Physical Abuse My First Boyfriend Did To Me?" Yes, while I was pregnant with twins, we had a physical fight, and it caused me to lose one of my babies. I had to raise that child, who had to lived without his father, because I had to leave the abusive relationship while I was 4month pregnant.

My story could be about how I felt after sixteen (16) years when my son's father showed up to be a part of his life. Or, I could talk about him trying to destroy my son's mind by telling him bad things about my family keeping him away. I thought, what about his father going to prison for (twenty-five) 25 years and the letters I was getting. Or, the phone calls he would make about rekindling our parenting relationships after 24 years. These all could be great books. I said to myself, "This would capture everyone's attention." My thoughts were, "Could this make me become a star writer..?" However, I feel I am terrible at writing. Placing my words on paper and putting the correct punctuation and proper words in the correct English form, really scares me. But, today I say I'm breaking the silence of all my fears! I'm going to tell you a story and express it in my own words. It will be how I talk, write and communicate. Here I go......

Hi, everyone! My name is Melinda. I am a believer of the Creator. I am a wife, mother, daughter, sister, aunt, niece, cousin, grandchild, friend, hair-stylist, hair-braiding teacher and a salon owner. I'm a woman that was hurting and don't know why. I've been on this earth for 43 years. I have experienced a lot, but at the same token, I haven't. I have a lot to learn and every day is a learning experience for me. I will take you on a journey from my present then my past. People say that the present is a gift. Which I do agree.

Every day I wake up and open my eyed, it is my present. It is the best gift from the Creator. No one can top that gift. I am not going to be all holy and spiritual with my story. Don't get me wrong. I do believe that there is a God. I do place my trust in the Creator. My family have different beliefs.
I grew up learning different religions. My people studied Baptist on my mom side. It was Sanctified on my father side. I attended Catholic school from 1st to 6th grade. My mom studied Jehovah for a short period of time. My husband's mom side studies Israelites and so on. I truly believe because I've experienced all these religions that it has made me have an understanding of them all. Being understanding is who I am. Please don't confuse this as if I'm confused and I need to pick one or the one you believe. This is my wonderful make-up of who I am. I love my family and all the things that come with them. So, I teach my children the same.

"Thanks to the Creator." Saying that makes me be all that I am. It is "Breaking the Silence." You can be all of this and still be a wonderful person and still go through mentally, sexually and physically abused. With the belief that I have, I have faith that there is a God because without him I couldn't continue to be saner. It gives me the strength to not allow my challenges change me to make me mean an evil. You should do the same. I encourage you to live life as happy as you can. The gift of life isn't promised. So, appreciate your gift and treasure it every day. Just like I do. Time has been hard, uncomfortable sometimes, even unbearable but, I put one foot forward and lean towards a better day to come.

As I lay down in my bed, I realize that being abused is very hard to talk about. No one wants to show their weakness, especially placing it in a novel where anyone one can read. Everyone judges a book by its cover. Once the cover page is opened, then here goes more judgements. So, that why we as humans hide it and never talk about it. I have always been that person that talked about any and everything. I almost never held my tongue. If you knew me, you would be like, "Wow, Melinda did you just say that?" I am the person who says what you probably are thinking to say. If it is on my mind, it is on my tongue, then in the air and going into whomever ears was close by. So, as I write this, please remember that this is hard for me. The closer I get to the abuse reveal, the more and more my heart get heavy and the softer my eyes get. I start blinking like crazy; like when it's raining hard outside and you're driving in your car; turning the windshield on high but, it's never enough rain in this storm for high windshield motions. As I continue to write, the blinking of my eyelids are uncontrollable. My toes are jumping as I write this. I'm in a fetal positing in my bed, looking for a secure space in my mind. My fingers are getting shaky as I write this in my bed, on my cellphone. I HAVE TO CLOSE MY EYES AND TAKE A DEEP BREATH.............. let myself cry and tell myself over and over again, Enough is Enough, repeatably.

"Enough is Enough............. I'm breaking this code. It's not just for me. This could help someone else."

Ok ...... life has taken me through some sh*t I didn't ask for. None of these circumstances was planned. I have been raised to respect people, even if they don't respect me. I feel that was the wrong way to teach a child growing up. I'm only five (5) generations from slavery. My grandparents were taught not to talk back. They told their children not to address adults with questions of Why, What, When, etc. So, from generation to generation more and more people are being abuse by close family, friends and or love ones because their voices were shut. My voice was being silenced. I couldn't say the word lie or shut up. I felt I couldn't even express my feelings. I said enough, and I refuse to teach my children this way. If you know my children, they are respectful. But, they also ain't going to be bothered with anyone's bull. I never wanted them to be hurt by someone they loved and trusted. I always want them to break away from anything that was harming them mentally; damn sure, physically and never fu*!#ing sexually. I'm so honest about life, I can't believe it! Maybe because I've been hurt by so many people, and year after year it's a different person.

My husband doesn't even understand my story. I have never told him all of it. Maybe because I never express to him my deepest fears. So, day after day we disagree about stuff and I feel he will never get it. I will stop holding back my insecurities. I am, from this day forward, stopping people from hurting me. Now, I don't know how this would end. Like I told you earlier, every day is a present and I will break this past pain. I want to make a promise to myself that I will no longer allow anyone to hurt me. I will no longer allow anyone to take advantage of me. I will make a vow to myself that I will come first. I promise that I wont worry about how someone treated me because I will treat myself better. Moving forward, people around me will give me the glory because, I am worth it. This day things will change. I will love myself more and stop the abuse.
please take a vow with me.

GET A PIECE OF PAPER AND PUTTING THIS ON IT.

I (state your name) will no longer allow anyone to hurt me...
I (state your name will no longer allow anyone to take advantage of me.
I (state your name) vow to myself that I will come first.
I (state your name) promise that I want worry about how someone treat me because I will treat myself better.
I (state your name) moving forward will make people around me to give me the glory, because I am worth it.

This day things will change.
I (state your name) will love myself more and stop the abuse.

70

At the age of 16, I was sexually assaulted by a man that I was meeting for the first time. My girlfriend that lived on my block was introducing me to a boy that she knew. She told me that he was coming over and I waited all day excited to meet this guy. I didn't know too much about him. Only what she had told me. You know the usually (cute, hot a car and but, he didn't live in the neighborhood.) This was perfect for a young girl, like myself, that was naive. Not knowing that this would be dangerous to be hooked up with a friend of a friend that you don't know. I only knew his nickname. So, all day he was coming over but never did. He kept saying was coming. So, when it got dark she went home and so did I.

Then late, about 11pm, he called her then she called me. He never called my number or even ask me what's my number. As I think about it now this was a setup for what really went down. Anyway, she called and told me that he was outside and told me to come and meet him. I told her, "Girl naw. My mom isn't going to let me come out its late." She suggested that I sneak out the back door come down the alley and come to her house. I didn't not think about anything but, how exciting it was that he came to see me. I didn't just at that moment, it took a minute to get myself together. I arrived at her house and he was sitting in his car. She and I walked to his car and she introduced us. We talked for thirty (30) minutes then he invited me to get in his car. My girlfriend friend got restless and left to go in her house because she was cooking her some food. I stayed and continued our conversation. Before I knew it, he placed the running car in drive, and took off. I asked, "Where you going? I can't go to far." He said, "I'm just going to park a little out the street lights"; which the street lights were beaming down into the car. I felt safe. He drove down a little towards a dark spot on my block telling me that it will be ok. He said he didn't want people who were walking pass to look into the car. Which I was not disagreeing but, not agreeing either. It was a lot of street walkers even though it was like a little pass midnight. So, we talk more and more.

Meanwhile, my mom was in the house not knowing I snuck out the house. She fell asleep and I was out just talking. After talking for so long, I said to him, "Okay, it was cool talking to you. I'm about to go in because it is getting late; and I know my mom is a night walker. If she wakes up and I'm not in my bedroom she is going to freak out." So, he said, "Okay, let me drive you back", even though I was in walking distance from my door steps. I said, "No need, I can name it." Then he started getting aggressive saying, "Well let's just talk more." Then he stared rubbing on me and then I was cool. But, then he began to go too far. With his hands, he was trying to take my clothes off. I told him "No", but it wasn't what he wanted to hear. He was telling me how cute I was and that he really like me, and we could be a cut couple, if we spend more time. I was then afraid because his hands were like an octopus all over me. He was not listening and when I said, "Stop!", he did. He then said, "Okay, I understand. Do let me just take you home." So, instead of me getting out, he placed the car in drive and said he was going around the block to drop me off like a man should do. He said, "When you're out with me, I will treat you like a lady." Which it was the right words at the right time. I agreed for him to drive me around the block. But, when he was supposed to make that right turn to go to my house, he didn't. He took me too far from my house. I begged him to take me home. Knowing that my mom didn't know I was gone, and my friend didn't come back out. He knew he had the upper hand. I was young and not a fast thinker. I got scared and demanded to be brought home. He then stopped the car next to an apartment building telling me this is where he stayed and it ok for me to chill with him. I didn't agree all. All I wanted to do is to go home.

His hands became a spider, octopus and it felt like I couldn't move my hands fast enough pushing his strong body off of me. It was like a dream. It was like I wasn't even there. I didn't pay attention to which direction he drove. I wasn't familiar of this area. It was like I was out of space and couldn't get home because I didn't know which way to go. All the while, I was thinking I'm going to open the door and get out. He then pulled out a gun and that just paralyzed me. I was crying and asking him why was he doing this. Why did he take me away from my block? Asking him not to kill me. The then threatened me and told me to take my pants down and I refuse with, "No. no. no." Then he placed the gun to my head and told me again with force. I didn't. He started doing things with my body that I didn't agree with. He had placed the gun in between the seats as he got on top of me, then he taped me. All I can do was just cry. He had no condom on. All I could do is pray. I prayed not to catch Aids, HIV, or any sexually transmitted disease. I prayed, yes that he takes me home and that I be alive and safe. All while he was rapping me.

I didn't even know his name, how old he was, what was his life like or even if I was the first person he did this to. Was there someone else he rapped before me. These were the strange thoughts that were running through my mind. I kept telling him to "Stop, please", but he wouldn't. This all happened in the front seat of his passenger car. I was so hurt and ashamed of what the position I put myself in. Thinking about what if I didn't sneak out? What if I didn't get into the car? What if I wasn't so thirsty to have a man tell me all these nice and beautiful things? I thought about turning the clock around like this didn't happened. But, it was real.

This was really happening, and I had to accept it. Once he was done doing his business, it was over.

As a young, inexperienced girl, all the small details never crossed my mind. A very important prayer, I prayed was to not to get pregnant. This man didn't even bother to take out his privacy out when he released himself. I was mad when I realize that I could get pregnant from this. It came to me later as he started driving me home. I thought about my eighth (8th) grade teacher Mrs. Johnson. She told us, the girls, about a time when she was not at school and why she was out for a while; why she had bruises on her face. Her talk she gave the class was about the time she was leaving school. She was attacked by a man in the gangway. She fought for her life. She told us that sometimes it easy to attack them back, but it's much easier to just let them do what they are trying to do, just so you can live the next day. She told us that he dragged, kicked, stabbed, punch and rapped her; while she was fighting back. But, when she no longer had strength to fightback he gave up and ran. She told us that sometimes it ok to feel weak so, they can feel strong, just so you can live for tomorrow. So, I did just that. I gave in and let him do what he had planned to do. Mrs. Johnson had come to school and still ran the class like a strong black woman. I admire her that she didn't let this destroy her. Watching her in (eigth) 8th grade going through, is what kept me strong with my attack.

When I made it home I ran up the stairs to my house and cried out to my mom. I told her I was sorry and I shouldn't have left out. I then explained to her what happened. She called the police and they rushed me to hospital. I was bleeding, in shocked and in pain. Test were done. The Morning After-Pill was given, and I was evaluated. Being asked questions over and over again about what happened was not something I wanted to do but, I had to. Every time I had to explain, it was painful. But we wanted to catch this person. I didn't have a lot of information on this guy. I gave them all what I knew which was, nothing. My friend, who I thought was my friend, didn't have nothing to say, either. She said he was a friend of a friend and couldn't help. I was so worried that I could be like my teacher pregnant, but with no husband. And, not knowing, because I had to wait to make sure that the morning after pill worked. Long story short I wasn't. Months went by trying to forget this ever happened trying to live life as normal as possible; being a strong black woman. Which I have done. I forgave and years later, I forgot, and I moved on. How?

I moved on with prayer and self-love. My mom said this was done and it's over let's move from this and never talk about it. You know what? I did this for years. It hurt more and more keeping this pain inside. I was so angry at my mom. Well I should not have been, it wasn't her fought. But, I still was. I never got help to deal with this, so, I allowed people, after people to hurt me sexually, mentally physically and emotionally. Until one day I went to therapy to talk to someone about my attack. To understand that it wasn't my fought. That my decision to go meet someone wasn't what I deserved.

Talking to someone about why you having issue is good thing. Being angry at my mom wasn't going to remove this pain. Over the years I became more and more angry at her that no matter what she did or said. I had my guards up, until now.

After 27 years My silence is broken.

I forgive.....

Melinda Chervil Cobb Bio

Melinda Chervil Cobb is a wife and a mother of four super talented children. She's a Chicago native, born and raised on the southside. In 1992, she graduated from Calumet High School, attended University of Chicago and graduated with Honors in 2012, from Dudley's Beauty College. She is a Master Stylist with a concentration on healthy and natural hair growth. She is the CEO/Owner of Nywele Hair Salon, Incorporated. She is a licensed hair braiding teacher, licensed cosmetologist , Bronner Brother Consultant and a former independent contractor within the Chicago education system, where she taught underprivilege youth techniques of braiding and maintaining healthy hair. She is also a proud member of Alpha CHI PI OMEGA SORORITY and fraternity of Illinois. Every day, Melinda is leaving her imprint in the world by teaching others to love, be themselves and live a natural-beauty life through her professional and personal experiences

Chapter 8

Plagued by Failure,
You Will Never Amount to Anything!

(Fasting and Going From Glory to Glory)

By LaDonna Mitchell (Horne)

"Worlds are expanding making room for you!"

Plagued by Failure, You Will Never Amount to Anything!

(Fasting and Going From Glory to Glory)

Where Doubt Was Born

"Some of YOU will never make it out of high school. You will be **HIGH SCHOOL DROPOUTS**. And some of YOU will be pregnant before you even graduate from high school." Those were the painful words spoken to me by my beloved eight grade Z-Group Teacher, Mrs. L. She would literally stand at the head of our small class with her crisp white blouse and long blue skirt; a halo of beautiful soft brown curls hung like a bouquet of flowers around her head. She was an African American woman with a pale white complexion, maybe in her late 40s to early 50s at the time. I absolutely adored this lady on one hand and deeply resented her on another. I admired her success, she was successful to me because she didn't live in the projects. She dressed well and always looked perfect in my eyes. She was extremely articulate and well-liked by her fellow teachers. I looked up to her because she was an educator and a very smart one at that. She had to be the best, because she was the leader of the Z-Group.

The Z-Group consisted of a small crew of high scoring standardize test taking children who lived in the Cabrini Green Housing Project and attended Richard E. Byrd School. Our School Richard E Byrd was an inner-city K-8th Chicago Public School. The Z-group was formed to supplement learning for a few kids who were consider some of the smartest kids in the school. We were told we were in the Z-Group because we were at the top. We were taught on subjects that were considered above our grade level. We believed we were special, because we were escorted away from the regular classroom setting to another class to do additional higher level learning as well as extra-curricular activities.

This particular teacher was someone I held in very high esteem. But she continued to tell us on a regular basis that we would never amount to anything in life. Hearing her say these things made my blood boil at times and then other times it made me shrink down lower in my chair. It choked my confidence at times and other times it made me fiercely determined to make her out of a liar. Now that I think back on those times, I don't recall ever discussing the issue with my mother or anyone else in authority, for that matter. I simply internalized her statements and her words created this bitter battle inside of me. Constantly waging war within were two forces: my young and naive inner drive to be successful and the coward who would consistently remind me that it was too hard to be success and be the best and that I should just resign myself to being ordinary.

I really don't know where the idea of trying to be the best first showed up in my life, but it always seemed to be a struggle. I recall joining the girl scouts and there was a painful episode where I was given the task of committing to memory the girl scout oath. For the life of me, I could not remember that oath. I sat in the chair totally defeated. I fumbled through tears to recite this oath:

On my honor, I will try:
  To serve God* and my country,
  To help people at all times,

It was like they were pulling my teeth. I cried and cried hoping they would just let me slip by. I don't recall if the girl scout leaders let me slip by, but I did continue to be involved. But that was one of my earliest memories or just being ordinary, not putting forth much effort, not giving my all to be the best and it served me well because I failed miserably. I absolutely hated being a failure. I hated with a passion getting bad grades and doing poorly in anything. But my confidence level was so low. I had no one cheering for me from the sidelines. I had no one telling me I was a winner. Or maybe someone was, but I just wasn't turned into that voice. I would learn later in life, that sometimes you have to tune into the right channels to get the right messages. I would learn later that we have power over what messages we allow in our life. But very early on, I was getting the wrong messages from people of great influence in my life.

Eventually, being the best and being a person of excellence became a part of my personality as I grew into a teenager; and I started attending Lincoln Park High School, church on a regular basis, and started attending a Christian Club called, Young Life. Many of the people I encountered on a regular basis helped to re-enforce certain values and beliefs in my life. God had a plan for my life. But, there were still those chilling voices questioning my value, still trying to convince me that I was worthless and would not be successful. Women at church saying "You are from the projects, how can you afford to carry a Gucci bag, where did you get those coach bags? You see my mom often took me to shopping on the Magnificent Mile, Michigan Ave. Sometimes church folks can be as cruel as the people outside the church. They would say the worst things in the nicest voice and the biggest smile. Church hurt can be painful and damaging. But again, God had a plan!

 For God has not given us a spirit of fear, but of power and of love and of a sound mind.
*In the Kingdom there is no such thing as a dead end job, life, relationship etc. The workplace is a perfect breeding ground for all kinds of success.
All life has value, and God purchased our worth on the cross. In fact, our lives were so valuable to him, he purchased ours by giving HIS!

Worlds Are Expanding Making Room For You

I remember one of the first times I had an encounter with the glory of God. I was working at CSU and I was seeking to be promoted by my supervisor at the time. She was the director of Human Resources and I was acting as her administrative assistant. Whatever assignment she gave me, I did it. Even things that were outside my job description, I did, running to get the entire HR staff lunch, I did, it didn't matter what she assigned to me I did it with a smile.

One day I went to talk to my supervisor about being promoted and possibly making more money. She basically told me it wasn't going to happen, no special reason, it just wasn't going to happen. So in my discouragement, I went running to God crying and all upset. I said "God you said in your word to do everything as unto the Lord and that's what I have been doing and this lady still won't give me a raise or a promotion. The Lord spoke to my heart and said "you are absolutely right to do everything as unto me. It's not your boss that you want to please it's ME! Do your job with a spirit of joy and a heart of praise. Perform your duties with a spirit of Godly excellence. Always do your very best work. Seek my face for creative ways of doing your job. Dedicate your day to me when you rise. Start your day with prayer and praise and worship. Find scriptures that line up with your desires and confess those over your life daily. Don't ever leave me out of the equation." The scripture says Promotion doesn't come from the east or the west but from the Lord. God anticipates promotion for you. God desires that you grow naturally and spiritually. He decreed promotion for you in his word. He said in
◄ Jeremiah 29:11 ►

"For I know the thoughts that I think toward you, saith the LORD, thoughts of peace, and not of evil, to give you an expected end."

Then In 3 John 1:2 the word says, "Beloved, I wish above all things that thou mayest prosper and be in health, even as thy soul prospereth." God was encouraging my heart to continue being the best person ever. This was one of a few first lessons where God spoke directly to me. He wanted me to fully understand that no one in this world validates my existence! HIS opinion of me is the only one that is always of the utmost importance! He helped me to understand that what they say about me or think about me will never fully determine MY DESTINY.

He wanted me to not be weary in well doing for in due season I would reap if I didn't faint. Well I did do just that and before I knew it, I was in church one Sunday morning and the pastor said a miracle is going to happen this week. I said well oh OK, praise God! Went to work, was sitting at the front desk and the chief of police came up and asked for my supervisor, I said she

81

was in her office. He went directly into her office and escorted her out of the building. She had been FIRED. Then the next thing I knew was that I was being promoted to Assistant HR Manager with a 10% increase. Praise God!!! He MIRACULOUSLY did what he had promised.

Proverbs 27:17Amplified Bible (AMP)

As iron sharpens iron, So, one man sharpens [and influences] another [through discussion].

Surround yourself with other people of God at work, at home and at church. Link up closely with like-minded people. People who are walking by faith not by sight.

Lazy men make excuses, people who are hungry for success make a way. People often say I can't find no jobs, all the good jobs are taken. Proverbs 26:13 "The slothful man saith, There is a lion in the way; a lion is in the streets." In this scripture, the lion in the street was his reason to be fearful. But, God gave David the ability to kill a lion with his bare hands. This man was slothful both naturally and spiritually. He refused to exercise his faith knowing that if he made some moves, God would make some moves on his behalf. Faith takes courage.

God has taught me to assess my skills and put them to great use, assess my environment, determine where my skills will command the most money. He taught me that I have dominion in the earth over all the animals, fish and birds. We tell things in the earth what to do. We speak to the universe in the mighty and in the matchless name of Jesus and we say job opportunities come to me, DOORS OPEN FOR ME!

I remember being unemployed during a period in my life where my children were school aged and I needed some extra money while looking for a full time job. Well I noticed that some of the young people in the neighborhood liked to have their hair braided and that was a skill I had developed from my youth braiding my own hair and my daughter's hair. I decided I would braid hair and get paid for it. It wasn't the most glamourous job, but it helped me to bring in some extra cash for miscellaneous household items and school lunch. There was another time I was underemployed and needed to work a part time job. So I found a job on the weekend doing food sampling events. It required me to talk to the public and hand them samples of different food products. The pursuit of the presence of God is both a goal and a mark of spiritual maturity.

In 2012 I moved to Phoenix AZ, and I had my little girl and a small one-bedroom apartment. I was there about a month, going on job interviews, fasting and praying. One day I remember crying to God saying, "Oh Lord, I don't understand why I don't have a job and I don't understand this and that!" And, I recall him distinctly saying to me, "Quit crying and worship me!" Hallelujah! Well I immediately changed my speech and started saying, "Lord I thank you for my new job! I thank you Lord and I praise you! You are worthy of all the praise, and the honor and the glory! You are Holy, you are Great! You are marvelous!" Well within a couple of days I had received a call from a former co-worker and Director of mine, he informed me that a former colleague from GSU was looking for me and wanted to offer me some employment. I was overjoyed, thinking God you came through for me. What I learned was that crying and complaining was not the correct way to get God's attention. While God is sensitive to our cry, he responds to praise and worship. Praise was the portal to the passage way of blessings from God! Praise was also a tool to defeat Satan's trap of depression and defeat in and over my life. When you complain and cry even to the Lord, it is a reflection of fears presence in your life. Fear is counterproductive in the Kingdom of God.

Small Victories Created Great Faith

I also recall while working at UIC in the very beginning that some of the managers had student workers who worked for them. I had quite a bit of responsibility and thought it would be nice to have someone to help. So, I approached my supervisor and asked if I could hire a student worker. She immediately said no. I went home prayed about it and the next day, she said I could go ahead and hire a student to help me with some of my duties.

Another time in the very early part of my career there, I noticed that many of the staff carried laptops. I again approached my boss and asked her if I could have a laptop. She said no, what did I need a laptop for. I told her to do work at home that I couldn't finish at work. She said no again, you don't need a laptop. I went home, prayed about it and within a couple of days she came back to me saying she was going to order a laptop for me.

God Valued me: Going from Glory to Glory

While at UIC, I continued to receive supernatural increases that took me from glory to glory. These blessings usually manifested during periods of fasting and prayer or shortly after. The very first time it happened I was asking God how to gain an increase. He led me to apply to a job opportunity on campus at UIC. I was called to an interview with three women. They moved me forward to the next phase which involved interviewing with the Director of the unit. She announced at the end of the interview that she liked me and that I should be hired. That next day I received a call from Central HR saying I had been offered the job with a $5000 increase. I immediately informed my new boss in my then current job that I was offered a new position and was leaving. She was new to the job herself and she didn't want to lose me. So, she said what would it take for me to stay. I told her that the new department was offering $5000 in my new role. She said she would match it. Meanwhile Campus HR had called back to let me know that the new job was a lateral move and no increase could be given for lateral moves. I was devastated, but God was like just wait, don't say anything. So, I waited and as promised. My new manager put the paperwork in place to increase my salary by $5000. Once again, I experienced the glory of God by way of a supernatural increase and as a result of fasting and prayer.

A couple of year later, the glory of God yielded the next supernatural increase which came while on a fast. One day at work, I received an email asking me to apply for a Human Resources Officer job at the Illinois Student Commission. The job was a step lower than my title of HR Associate, but I said "What the heck, I'll apply anyway, and I felt the urging of the Holy Spirit to apply, so I did. The first step was clicking a button to express my interest in the position. Shortly thereafter, I received an email from the Hiring manager asking me to complete the online application and come in for testing. The hiring manager was trying to find her replacement. She was leaving the organization to own and operate a Chiropractor Clinic.

I was a little nervous about the testing process, but somehow by the grace of God, I did well enough to be called in for an interview with the HR Director and two of her other staff. The interview with the HR Director was very interesting because I really don't recall talking about my credentials as much as I remember talking about shopping and other non-interview type things. They asked what kind of salary I was looking for I said I wanted $59,000. The interview ended with them promising to call me once a decision was made sometime the next week.

Well the next week went by and I had not heard from the director, so I called to follow-up. She said she would call me back and that she was in the middle of something. I waited patiently for her call and when she finally did, she offered me the position with a salary of $60,000. I gladly accepted because that was more than I had asked for. Additionally, my seniority with the state would continue in terms of my vacation accrual rates and my time with the retirement system would not be affected.

Well, once I got off the phone with the HR Director, I praised God like crazy and then I went into my boss's office to give her the good news. She was somewhat aware of the situation because I had used her as a reference. So, she kind-of knew that I would get the job. Once I confirmed the offer to her, she said " I can't afford to let you leave...what would it take for you to stay? I was a little shocked and thrown off by her statement. So, I just pulled a number out of my head. Before I knew it, I said, "$10,000 and I want to be able to work from home twice a month." She replied... OK! I said Okay! We stood there like two people ready to go to war. Well after waiting about 4 weeks for her to put in the paperwork and for the transaction to increase my salary of $58,024 by $10,000 finally got approved by HR. Hallelujah! Once again, God had moved my situation and increased my salary supernaturally all as a result of fasting and prayer.

LaDonna Mitchell (Horne) Bio

LaDonna Mitchell-Horne is a wife, mother of four, HR professional, Employment Coach and now Author. She is currently employed and works remotely as a Human Resources Associate with a major university located in Chicago. She holds a Master's degree from Governor State University in Communications, Human Performance and Training and received her Bachelor's degree from Western Illinois University. She recently relocated to Dallas Texas. She gave her heart to Jesus at the tender age of 14 and has been learning to trust him more and more ever since. She shares her testimony and faith in Jesus with most everyone she comes in contact with. Her favorite scripture is found in Mark 11:24: Therefore, I say unto you, whatsoever things you desire when you pray believe that you receive them and you shall have them.

Chapter 9

You Are No Longer Welcome Here!

By Veronica Howard

"HELP should never diminish HOPE"

You Are No Longer Welcome Here!

As a kid I always attended church, with my Mom and little sister. I was raised in a house of constant prayer. My mom prayed every day at 7:00 PM until 8:00 PM, since I could remember. One time I asked her did she pick that time. She said the number 7 represent completion. The number 8 is very significant, too. The number 8 represents new beginning! Not only was she a praying woman, but she was very disciplined and obedient in the Lord. I watched my Mom pray, praise, worship, and most of all listen to God. She did His will. I watched her trust God do the impossible! Yes, I saw how she prayed. We always had food on our table and clothes on our backs. And yes, I heard the rent man give her a few days more to pay the rent. And, the insurance man would come back the following week to collect the insurance payments. I got it! I saw her blessings and I heard of God's power but, to step out of the natural into the supernatural is something that I feel once you experience this, you will never want to go back. Because, when life takes you on another path, you cannot always depend on Grandma and Mommy prayers. There comes a time, when now you have to have your own personnel relationship with God.

The beginning of my new beginning. Yes I said it!

I will never forget the day that I was first diagnosed with Cervical Cancer; one of the number one killers of African American woman. That day, I had an outer body experience. I totally felt my brain leave my head and my arms and legs just moving to get out of this body that was now ill. At the time I felt defeated, numb, sick, lost, scared and confused. I felt like I was in the twilight zone. My inside screamed "Help" and "NO" at the same time. It was unbelievable. As a child and then teenager and then Adult, I never had as much as a cold. And now my pathologic report confirmed that I had the "Big C". Never knew that this would be a new chapter in my life. You see my doctor made it seem like a piece of cake. He said all he had to do, was go in me and take out my uterus, then I would be good. Not knowing this will become a two-year battle.

It was July 28, 2015. It was a nice summer day. I had a 10:00 AM appointment with my GYN doctor. Previously, I had seen the doctor about 3 to 4 times about the same pain I had on the left side bottom of my stomach. I had this pain for many years and when I was going to the doctor they use to give me colposcopies.

Colposcopies are a procedure they give you when you have abnormal pap smears and they find abnormal cells that if untreated could cause Cancer, after transferring to another Health Insurance company. I got another doctor and I explain to him all of my pass medical history and I'm quite sure he received my medical report. But, he just ignored me and kept telling me I am fine.

(Ladies and Men: Just keep in mind if your doctor don't listen to you, IMMEDIATELY leave and get another doctor. Early prevention is Key & A Must! I cannot stress it enough.)

I wanted to transfer back to my old insurance but, I decided just to find a new doctor. Before I could tackle this, I found out I was sick with the "Big C". Yep Cancer of the Uterus.

I just kept putting it off because I had a job that I couldn't really take off. And the times I took off, I had to tend to my kids. I had to take them to their doctors' appointments or, handle business at their schools. As a single parent, I had to do what I had to do.

Every time I would go the doctor, he would say I had a urinary tract infection. After taking medicine for the same diagnoses, I decided to be more persistent and let the doctor know that it had to be something else. I had a discharge with this terrible odor and knew at this point it had to be something more serious than a urinary tract infection. The doctor finally did a biopsy and the report showed that I had Cervical Cancer of the uterus. The doctor referred me to an oncologist, my appointment was in August 2015. As I left the doctors that day I was in total shock, me not thinking how serious this was for some reason in my mind, I down played it. I felt fearful, numbness, and just a feeling of emptiness. I did not know what was expected to be next. I sat in my car in the parking lot of the hospital and decided I was not going to tell my family or so-called friends. See, I wasn't always liked a lot growing-up, because I had a hot mouth. Therefore, I was not going to let anyone take advantage of me. I was an angry little girl coming up, in the red district zones, where people tried to take advantage of you. I was not having it!

Knowing my family did not love me or they did not care. I wasn't telling nothing. See I come from a family who is divided. No real love, no cookouts, no family dinners, no phone calls from anyone just to say Hi if you are in the hospital; no calls or visit unless they think you are dying or you are dead. My cousins' associates with females who do not like me and even tried to get me hurt. So, I thought, why share this with a family who will do that? I feel that if you don't like my sister, you can't like me. That's a given, but not in my family. I never really been through a lot of hardships; except bills being behind, a man cheating on me, friends turning on me. You know the basic things that happens in life that we think are so bad, when really it is not. They are only trials and tribulations; that I was taught as kid that we will go through.

After seeing the oncologist, I was told that all I have to do is have a surgery that consist of removal of my cervix, and the Cancer would be gone and I will be fine. I was then upset saying to myself I wanted another baby. But at the age of 45, I wondered if I was really thinking logically? Or, did I just wanted to play down what was really going on. But, then at the same time telling the doctor it is ok, my health first.

During this time, I started a relationship with a friend who was incarcerated. He told me he would be there for me. He was at the time but, later find out infidelity and addiction later played a key role in our break up! I never had someone to take care of me and I just knew he loved me because he was wiping my butt and taking me to the hospital. He was there mentally (at least I thought so), physically and so on. My family wasn't there, so I thought just his presence meant he LOVED ME. Wow! Was I in for a rude awakening; even his mom came to visit me in the hospital and called me on the phone. I thought that was love because again I didn't know what loved looked like. I so loved his mom. I thought she was the coolest mom I ever met; to later find out that she would take up for her son rather it hurt him or not. Prior to us getting together he lost his brother, so maybe she held on because that was all she had left.

When I started telling him to get a job, pay bills and get off drugs to pay for my car he totaled in an accident, she became mean to me. I guess she was thinking I was being mean but, as a man he supposedly, made his wrongs right. I truly wished the best for him and I was hoping he got a job and kept it, continue going to church and became a better man. I truly saw something great in him that maybe one day it will manifest. So there Another HURT! On top of me fighting for my life, I was fighting for his life, too. Not only was I feeling lonely and scared, but I was looking for love and comfort as well.

After having the surgery October 8, 2015, the doctor told me I had to have 25 rounds of radiation and chemotherapy as well. My first surgery I had was robotic surgery. This was a new procedure that the doctor said was going to work instead of having to be cut open. But, it did not go wel. So, then I had to have surgery again which was in November of 2015. This time they had to cut me open and I was a little nervous, but I knew that I will put my trust in the Lord.

So, I prayed the Prayer of Protection:

Psalms 91 "He that dwells in the secret place of the most high shall abide under the shadow of the Almighty. I will say of the Lord, He is my refuge and my fortress: my God; in him will I trust. Surely, he shall deliver thee from the snare of the fowler, and from the noisome pestilence."

God was the only One that could help me at this time. As a child, I was taught that God will protect, heal, and confront you; so now I knew it was time to live on God promises and trust in Him whole heartily.

My mind kept saying, "Do I trust him enough that he heals me? Do God hear my prayers? Why would he listen to me; a Sinner who fell down? I was living in the world and going to church on Sunday. So,now my mind set was all over the place. I thought things like am I saved enough? Do God hear me? Why would he listen to my ungodly self?

Then I read Psalms 37, 25-26

"I have been young, and now am old; yet have I not seen the righteous forsaken, nor his seed begging bread. And this was confirmation to me that God is who He says He is. "

I started the treatment which had me sicker than what I expected. I got so burnt between my legs, all in my vaginal area, between my buttocks, all in my private area; the whole nine yards, and inside of my vagina as well. The doctor decided to stop my treatment. I was down to the last three treatments and could not complete them. I was in too much pain, and they stop the treatment to see if the burning will have gotten better. The burnt areas between my thighs on my private area got worst and worst and I was confused because I was no longer doing the treatment. I was instructed by the radiation doctor to take sitz bath which consist of soaking in water baking soda and Epsom salt for 15 minutes 3 times a day, after a while these baths started not to work. I was up all night crying my boyfriend at the time use to hold me and tell me everything will be alright.

It was terrible, I later started staying with my mom and she told me to make an appointment at the burn unit at the nearby hospital. After going there and getting some powder for burns that soon stop working as well the doctor couldn't believe how bad I was burnt, she said if I was burnt that bad on the outside she could only imagine how bad I was on the inside. After she explain to me that the outside will heal as well as the inside but the inside will take much longer. I continue to take the medicine and prayed.

I was due to go to the doctor in June 2016. To get checked to make sure the Cancer did not come back or spread. When I went in I saw a lady doctor who just gave me a pap smear and told me that they didn't see no signs of Cancer. I was lost because prior to these doctor appointments the oncologist told me I will have to do a CT cat scans to check to make sure the Cancer didn't come back. The CT scan is a procedure where they look in your body to make sure no Cancer growth has return. A pap smear couldn't show that information. But at the time all this was new to me. Not only was I afraid but, I was fighting for my life as well trying to learn about Cancer itself. The doctors didn't detect any Cancer with the pap smear.

I later started having stomach aches from July 2016 all the way up August 2016. Again, I was in and out of the hospital and they keep telling me the pain was a small bowel obstruction. They kept giving me pain medication and kept me in the hospital for 3 to 5 days. Then I finally, I got sent to another hospital, where the doctor told me and my family there was nothing else they could do for me and told my mom and my eldest child to take me home and make me comfortable to die. The doctor told me and my family I had only months left to live. I knew then at that moment that I needed God. They started the process to send me to hospice, my mom who is a praying woman, did not take the doctors report so lightly. My daughter and mom called John Hopkins because my mom said this is what the spirit spoke to her and said. Thank you Holy Spirit! I knew God had the last word. My mother told me to get dressed to go to another hospital outside of town, (John Hopkins)

At this point, an over calming spirit came over me. I knew then I had to put all my trust in God. At that moment I was stuck between "Oh Lord" and "Thank you Jesus". Because right then, I knew whichever way things went, God had my back! If I stayed on earth and beat this battle, He was not finished with me or, He had work for me to do. If I didn't expire, I knew He needed me more.

I became so ill that I was fine with that, and then on the other hand I was not finished living. I prayed day in and day out asking God to spare my life, I told God that I want to see my kids grow up and watch my grandbaby grow into a man, so I could see his kids as well.

I was always taught that God will speak to you and as we rode to Baltimore; I knew that God was with me and had been carrying me all alone. You see; to go and get a second opinion I believe that brave of me because my second opinion could have been I am going to still die. But God spoke to my spirit and told me I was going to be fine. I just keep saying Okay God I am going to trust you even when I can't trace you.

Have you ever been in a life death situation and all you could do is pray and put all your trust in the Lord? Who else is there to run to in time of need? But my God. He is the only person that can help you. No one else. I hear folks say things like people run to God when they in trouble. I think it is okay, I've learned that one else can do me like Jesu. In life, you will learn to go to Him in your good times as well as your bad times. As you grow in Christ mentally and visually, you will begin to be delivered from things. It's a process. Things just don't happen overnight.

One day at a time sweet Jesus that's all I'm asking from You.

I knew as a child, life will keep happening. I was also taught that I was fearfully and wonderfully made, as my momma always told me. You see, I have a praying momma and grandma. So, if you need to call on the Lord in times of trouble go ahead and wait on the Lord. "HELP should never diminish HOPE." I called on Him and He was there all alone. "He will never leave or forsake you." I've learned that through my trials and tribulations. And, this fight that we experience are necessary. Sometimes, you go through certain situations to get you closer to God. If God want to use you, He will get your attention any means necessary.

Once I got to the new hospital emergency room with 2 car loads of family members, I was in pain and I was just lost. In one car, it was me and my boyfriend and my son. In the other car was my mom, my niece, and my daughter. Once we got there, they checked me in. I was in the waiting area for about 3 or 4 hours before they called me. Once I got to the back they couldn't draw my blood because I am a hard stick so finally a young lady came in and got my IV going and was able to take my blood. Once they gave me some pain meds and took me in the back I started to feel a little better. The doctor said to me that they will do their best to help me. He then ordered the staff to put a gastric suction tub in my nose down to my stomach. This relieved the pressure on my intestines, since they were blocked. I could not eat, so they hooked me up to an IV which feed me. I couldn't hold nothing down without vomiting or being in severe pain.

September 2016. I had my surgery. I was in surgery for like 6 or 7 hours. Once I came out of surgery my body felt like a train wreck, I never felt so much pain in my entire life, not only did they have to put a pick line in my arm which the pain is so excruciating even with pain meds the pain is still outrageous but as time moved on and the pain got worst and worst I just keep holding on to my faith, I keep saying to myself; God didn't bring me this far to leave me. The surgery was successful. So know I am not completely out of the woods. I am now in the hospital recovering but still borderline near death, see the medical report told the doctors one thing. My hair started to fall out and I was giving up. When I first started to lose my hair I was in the hospital and took my braids out and my hair was in my hands I laid on the floor feeling overwhelmed with DO MY GOD HEAR ME? I laid on the floor in the hospital bathroom and cried out to God. A nurse came in and laid on the floor with me. She held me and comforted me. See how God places people in the right place at the right time. I love the song, 'God will take care of you', by Le'Andria Johnson.

95

I began to pray every morning, thanking God for giving me another day. I got closer and closer to God, after being in the hospital for almost two months. I had tubes in my stomach to help my bowels and my food properly go down smoothly.

They say LOVE covers a multitude of things. With the love the nurses, doctors continuously showed me, helped me feel better. Soon, I was finally released to go home to start my healing process. It wasn't easy at first, but I keep trusting in the Lord and He kept me.

Coming face to face with God is a beautiful experience, to see and to feel His love is the most beautiful thing you will ever want to experience. God is who He says He is. He will never leave us or forsake us. Even though the doctors gave up on me and I was almost near death the experience, it was still great. It helped strengthen my faith. Without Him I would not be here to share this with you all.

No matter how bad things looks, my God is a healer. He is omnipotent. He is the Beginning and the Ending. The bigger the trials and tribulations the bigger the anointing. I thank my Lord and Savior for giving me a fresh start. As I live, I will always trust in the Lord and know that His grace is real.

Grace is something we don't deserve, but He gives it to us and it is something you cannot buy.

So, Lord I thank you for your Grace and your mercy and your undivided love.

Just remember if He did it for me, He will do it for you. He is my Rock! And I will praise the Lord until I die; no matter what tomorrow brings, I will trust in the Lord. He is who He says He is. Lord I thank you for my NEW BEGINNING.

Dear Cancer and Hurt, YOU ARE NO LONGER WELCOME!

Veronica Howard Bio

Veronica Howard is a four-time Cancer Survivor and a woman after God's own heart.

She resides in District Heights, Maryland. She unapologetically loves the Lord and has a heart for his people. Her life story is one of Courage, Faith the, Belief and Surrendering. She graduated from Strayer University in 2006 with an Associate degree in Business Administration. She is also an Amazon bestselling coauthor of book, Sharing our Prayers. She is a member of the "Daughters of the Most High" praise group.

Today, she is a Station Manager for the Washington Area Transit Authority. She is the Administrator of the Cancer Support Ministry at Mt Ennon Baptist Church in Clinton, Maryland; She mentors audiences, friends, coworkers, and family members who are currently fighting Cancer.

Chapter 10

She Said...No!

By Patricia (Shay) Cosey

"Don't settle for a life that you don't want to live"

She Said...No!

They say it's every little girl's dream to grow up, wear a beautiful dress that makes her look like a princess, and get married. To be quite honest, that was never a dream of mine. My aspirations were to go to college, get a degree and a well-paying job, but above all, make my momma proud. Weddings were far and few in my family and even by the time I had attended college, I had not been to one-single wedding. As I grew up, I watched my mother and my aunts live in domestic partnerships with men who were at least 10+ years older than them. Each of them calling themselves wifey but no wedding and sometimes not even a ring. As they would have their typical sister gatherings by playing cards, talking trash, and then eventually arguing with one another, there wasn't one gathering that they hadn't discussed their "hubby". I learned very quickly from those gatherings that even if you lived with a man, he better be paying that child support and you better not depend solely on him for anything. As a strong, black woman, you needed to know how to go out there and get it for yourself and make sure to take care of your kids.

That was the code, already subconsciously carved out for me and all I had to do was keep living and I would eventually walk in it. Although I entered college without consciously thinking about living out the code, in my sub-conscious it was only a matter of time before I would get a long-standing boyfriend, we would live together, I would play the wife role and have that mans' babies. I thank God for divine interventions! Although I had already been in church for a year, when I turned 19 years old, I had officially given my life to Christ. He was my comfort and to be honest, my moral standards were now set sky high! As I got familiar with church, I came to know those domesticated partnerships that I witnessed, were actually called "shacking up" in the church world. They were not goals, and I felt deceived! Being immature in Christ, I actually went around condemning people left and right for shacking up and having pre-marital sex. My zeal for God left me merciless to other and surely puffed up... but haven't you heard, pride comes right before a fall.

My condemnation strike came to a screeching halt after a sin of my own had produced a baby right before the start of my Junior year. What started out as causal conversations with an old high school friend, ultimately left me gut-wrenching nervous and taking a pregnancy test in my dormitory bathrooms. I was disappointed in myself, scared and embarrassed, but I was still not settling for the "shacked up" life. With my beautiful baby girl in my arms, I kept my eyes on the prize. I knew I wanted to be a wife and that I would be a great one. I didn't stay with my daughter's dad, but I still wanted a husband and another chance to build a family unit. I was never about to settle for one of those domestic partnership situations. I started dating after having my daughter and this time around I needed a man who loved God and who I didn't have to explain this abstinence thing to. Some time had passed and a guy I met earlier that year at Bible study asked me out. I said okay, but I told my friends I didn't want to go out with him. They told me my reasoning was petty and that I needed to go out and have fun. He turned out to be a nice guy. He paid for things, sent flowers every month and always sent sweet messages. Newly saved, he encouraged me to read my Word and he often showed up at bible study. I wasn't sold, but maybe he could be "the one" *someday*.

Then it happened. A few months later I was invited over to his place and I thought this would be great! I could actually hang out with a gentleman and have a great evening and I knew for a fact that I didn't have to worry about fornicating. I was wrong, not even hours into my visit, the moves were being put on me. I was so disappointed. I laid there in silence without an ounce of courage to say "no". I was afraid to lose a nice guy, but I was disgusted. I thought we were on the same page. He apologized the next day and promised we would do better. I believed him, but as the story would go, we fell time and time again. Often times we argued and disagreed but the remedy to that was to conform and give in and settle all the irritated emotions down. Sometimes I was a willing participant, but whether he knew it or not, most times I died more and more on the inside. This grieved my spirit so much. I wanted out. He was not living up to this godly example of the man I thought he was supposed to be and I wasn't being the obedient child of God that I wanted to be. I felt the hypocrite stigma stamped across my face. Some people may think I was being too hard on myself, but I had a strong, personal desire to be Holy. I felt like I needed *him* to lead us in the right direction. Each time I gave myself away to this boyfriend that was not my husband, I lost more and more respect for him and myself. I felt stuck in a situation where I wanted so badly to do right, but I also wanted so badly to appease him for fear that I would lose a "good" man. I was silenced, hoping and wishing that things would just get better on their own.

I would often tell him that we didn't have to force this relationship if it wasn't a fit. Everything looked good on the outside but on the inside, I was emotionally drained and spiritually deprived. One day the light bulb came on! How could I keep shoving the blame on him? I needed to take responsibility for the role I played in this and steer my life in the direction I wanted it to go. Waiting on him to match my fervor and desired goals was just an excuse and it was truly holding me back. I decided I wasn't having any more sex with this dude. He was either going to be a good Christian man as he professed to be, or I would leave. So, on his birthday, instead of the infamous "birthday sex" that is so highly expected, he got simple gifts, a cooked meal after class and a kiss goodbye that night. I personally felt victorious, but I could tell he felt unfulfilled. A month later he came crying, telling me he *almost* slept with his baby momma after venting to her about how disappointed he was on his birthday and how heartless I was previously being towards him. They brought themselves all the way up to the bedroom I her mother's house and as he reported, he walked away before they totally indulged. I thought to myself... "Excuse me... you did what?". This was my shot out of this relationship. All that "oh he's a nice guy, he's such a gentleman" mess was going in one ear and out the other now. He messed up and I could technically say he cheated. I was ready to take on life with just me and my baby girl. I didn't need a man and whenever my husband came, he would be a *real* man of God and I wouldn't have to compromise.

He apologized for days on end, and I forgave him rather quickly. I was mad, but I was low-key, happy that he had messed up. Even in forgiveness, I was prepared to chuck the deuces and move on. The hopeless romantic that he was, went into public display of his affection towards me with flowers and gifts. A month or so later he asked to come and chill with me and my daughter to have a simple movie night. Then, right as movie night was coming to a close, he proposed to me in my living room. I was stunned, no one had ever proposed to me before. I couldn't break his heart and say no, so I forced some tears out my eyes (because you're supposed to cry right?) and then I said "Yes". I was so lost. I could barely sleep that night, thinking about what I had just agreed to.

I waited a couple days and then I uploaded a picture of my engagement ring on social media and captioned it "I said YES!". I got flooded with comments, likes and congratulations! All of the attention felt good, but I was not happy. I struggled with being honest with him. Shortly after Christmas I found myself repenting yet again, and for the life of me I couldn't work up enough courage to just say no and stop this madness. I didn't want to be here, and I definitely didn't want to get married! I hated the dynamics of our relationship and I needed to stop kidding myself! I was ready to tell him.

I put off telling him more and more. He was excited about being married and I was nauseous nearly every day. The nausea became all too real and by the end of January, guess what? I was actually pregnant yet again! Now I felt like I *had* to stay with him. If I left him, who was going to want to marry me with TWO kids? To my best friends I contemplated abortion because I was so ready to be done with this relationship. I cried my eyes out, stretched out on my living room floor and I prayed to God that He would forgive my thoughts. I wondered how was I going to finish school and raise two kids? The Lord led me to Jeremiah 1:5. He was letting me know that He knew my baby before it was even in my womb! At that moment I knew it would be a boy and I knew I would name him Jeremiah. We continued to date my entire pregnancy. We set the wedding date to April 2014 and I tried my best to stay focus, so I could give my children the best life possible. I told myself *at least* I wasn't headed into a domestic partnership. *At least* he wanted to marry me, and I wouldn't just be a baby momma. I rested my nerves and settled my mind on those things, constantly saying to myself "just do it Shay!".

We welcomed our baby boy into our lives and had 6 months left until our tentative wedding day. I had a new job, school and the new baby to keep me focused. I was finally in my last year of college and I was determined to fin

103

ish strong. I began talking to my internship teacher about my apprehensions on getting married. She encouraged me to pray about it and let God's peace steer me in the right direction. I did just that. Every day I was still searching for answers, signs and clues to whether or not I should go forth with this marriage. He didn't know, or maybe he did. I told him again about not forcing the relationship because we have a baby but he assured me that the devil just wanted to break us apart.

I knew better. I knew it wasn't the devil, and I knew I didn't want to get married to him. Consulting with God often left me ready to call it off, but I was too afraid to hurt his feelings. I was wrecking myself trying to look happy and fulfilled. I struggled with my inner emotions that often had me wondering if something was wrong with me. Why couldn't I just be happy with a nice guy. With everything in me I knew this wasn't destiny. With the wedding only two weeks away, we put the finances together to book our honeymoon. I sat in my internship about to book it and I became sick to my stomach. I went home on my lunch break and broke down completely. I was scared to be embarrassed. I was scared to hurt this man's feelings and scared to let all of our family and friends down. I was deathly terrified to be a single mother of two. I was staring destiny right in the face and was being taunted by the devil at the same time. I screamed in agony on the living room floor of my apartment. "God if you don't help me with this I'll never tell him! Please give me strength!".

After crying out, I worked up the courage to at least send him a text message. I explained how I knew this was not the direction God was leading me in. For clarity he replied back in a message "Are we getting married or not?" I took a deep breath, wiped the water from the wells of my eyes and replied "No". He rushed home from work and tried to pin this thing on the devil, yet again. I shook my head "no" multiple times. I had finally did it y'all. I chose me, my happiness and my destiny over my fears. It was the hardest thing I had ever had to do, and it cost me everything! With deep embarrassment we cancelled the wedding and apologized to all of the guest. While I walked with shame and guilt on the outside, on the inside I felt a peace I hadn't felt in a long time.

I spent two years alone, deepening my relationship with God, and healing my heart from the pain and heartache that I caused it before I met my hus band. The process was not easy at all but as I look at my life now, *I was totally worth it.* Many nights, I was alone and tempted with the multiple passes from men who may have wanted me for my outward assets but really knew nothing about me. My best friends had a Memorial Day barbeque at their sister's house. My kids were with their dads and I was taking the time to clean up and reboot our apartment for their return. My friends encouraged me to come out the house and get some food. I went and after a while this guy walks in whom I had just seen about a month before and jokingly made a comment about how fine he was and how if he was single I would make him mine! What in the world was he doing there at that barbeque? I thought God was trying to be funny bringing him in there like that. He was holding a conversation at the table about wealthy black people and how we needed to look beyond the historic image of us as slaves. My nerves got bad and I wanted to leave, but not before giving everyone a hug, including him. I went home and did the self-talk thing because *geesh,* that man was fine and intellectual! I told myself "get it together Shay, you are not ready for dating!"

A few hours later, he friend requested me on social media and wrote me an inbox message asking "did you make it home safely?". Y'all should have seen me in that house. I threw that phone down, dropped to me knees and prayed! After praying, I paced the floor, shrieked with a nervous joy, blushed, cussed in excitement and smiled from ear to ear. I snuggled under my covers and began to reply back and forth in messages. I had to feel him out and he kept it so straight forward with me. He asked to take me out and I asked him why he wanted to do that. He stated that at this point in his life, he was only entertaining potential future wives and I looked like I might fit that category. I told him I was on a dating "time out" until I knew why I kept shutting people down. He kept asking questions. He wanted to know what I thought God created me to do in this world and why God made me a woman. He boldly stated that he could possibly be the answer to my prayers. This initial conversation between us was going somewhere I had never gone before. He was pre-screening me! We continued to talk and message each other and a few weeks later we actually exchanged numbers because he said he didn't like to be on social media messenger like that (which he wasn't lying because it still holds true to this day).

That night on Memorial Day, was the beginning of something so big and beautiful, even my own mind had not conceived it. This guy looked like a real-life thug on the outside, but was so deep, spiritual and intellectual on the inside. I kept a prayer life so tough because it felt like something didn't add up. My friends and family were wondering what in the world was I doing with *him* because I'm sure they all imagined that I would end up with some button-down shirt-Deacon in the church. I thank God for a personal relationship with the Father. I prayed, and I asked the Lord to guide me and not let me waste my time. I asked specifically about whether or not I should date him because he was a little rough on the edges, and I didn't want to end up getting myself stuck. The Lord told me that Roland belonged to him and that he possessed a heart of Gold. God literally sent me to 1 Samuel 16:7 that night and I was floored. I wept because I knew in my heart, God was sending me a message about Roland, there was indeed something special about him.

After that, I gained a whole new confidence in talking to him and allowing him into my life. I wanted to see what God saw. As his layers began to peel back, I was amazed at the Man of God I was looking at. He didn't come already packaged with a ministry title, false claims to be holy or a pulpit to preach from. He came rogue-like, raw and unfiltered. It was my own relationship with God that revealed things to me that could not be seen with the naked eye. After promising never to settle again, this time I took a chance and believed God.

Today, I am married to the man of my dreams! He is handsome, intelligent, honorable and loves God with all of his heart. Every great aspect of him that used to be hidden on the inside, now shines forth radiantly I his outward appearance as he grew stronger in Christ. Our souls aligned and we were both free to be who we really were in Christ. I am so glad I didn't settle. My husband loves my children like they are his own and works hard to make sure we are well cared for. It was foolish of me to think that God was able to prepare a husband for me because I was a single mom of two. The woman I was before didn't know how to provide self-care to herself. I didn't realize my worth and I didn't believe that God would fulfill his promises. That couldn't be any further from the truth. You and I are worth far more than rubies and we were bought at a precious price! Please don't die a slow and silent death for fear of exposing or letting someone else down. Break the code and go after your wildest dreams. Don't settle for a life that you don't want to live. There are pivotal moments in your life where you will find yourself staring destiny directly in the face, and in order to make it there, sometimes you just have to say "no" and trust God with the rest!

Patricia Shay Cosey Bio

Patricia "Shay" Cosey is a dedicated wife, mother and entrepreneur. On any given day, you will find her teaching, guiding, encouraging, and loving on the people she comes into contact with. Shay joyfully became married to her husband Roland Cosey, in 2017. With a Bachelor's Degree in Early Childhood Education and an undying love for children, she combined her passions with her gifts, and began her own business as a Belly Casting Artist for expecting mothers. Every day she replays her story, remembering her journey from single-mom of two, to happily married to the man of her dreams. She will never forget that in order to get there, she had to say "no".

Chapter 11
Surviving Miscarriage and Beyond

By Regina Franklin

"Clear life's hurdles and run your race!"

Surviving: Miscarriage and Beyond

Lord- it is me again, coming you to after you "I" thought "I" had it all together.

Living the life, I wanted to live... my way

Going and coming as I please, disrespecting the gifts you've given to me

Help me to <u>TRUST YOU</u>

Doing things that had no purpose or need almost living a life of the street, you know that creed

Help me to <u>TRUST YOU</u>

As the many conversations I had with you were for you to do something for me, asking you for minuscule things that don't have value

Help me to <u>TRUST YOU</u>

Somewhere in there MY way became the wrong way. My emotions and mental frame of mind was not of my own.

Help me to <u>TRUST YOU</u>

The enemy had taken over, leading me down this path and that path turning me left and right. My right mind was nowhere in sight.

Help me to <u>TRUST YOU</u>

I've been seeing the light at the end of the tunnel

Help me to <u>TRUST YOU</u>

Shaking the chains, wiggling out of the cuffs

Help me to <u>TRUST YOU</u>

I see the blood, I know the result

Help me to <u>TRUST YOU</u>

Crawling not walking toward you LORD. I'm not worthy of being upright

Help me to <u>TRUST YOU</u>

I feel something, a movement in my belly, knowing something is different

Help me to <u>TRUST YOU</u>

Kneeling I begin to rise..why?

Help me to <u>TRUST YOU</u>
After all I've done, everything I know you despise
Help me to <u>TRUST YOU</u>
Feelings of unworthiness is leaving, this feeling in my stomach isn't deceiving
Help me to <u>TRUST YOU</u>
Holy Spirit is moving, kicking and pushing
Help me to <u>TRUST YOU</u>
Pregnant with possibilities I always had
Help me to <u>TRUST YOU</u>
Standing up with strength I didn't know I had
Help me to <u>TRUST YOU</u>
Lord I am ready, ready to be a vessel help me to remove me and <u>TRUST YOU</u>

Narrative...

In the beginning, I thought being a "bonus" mom was all I was going to be, and you know, I was fine with that. The day we took a test and realized we were having a baby. The shock of it all. The joke between my husband and I about how this happened.

To me, pregnancy is the most beautiful experience a woman can have. The announcement, the congratulations from everyone. Food never tasted so good, LOL!   Feeling the baby move. Seeing the ultrasounds. Hearing the heart beating. That is a euphoric feeling...

Until.... the pain starts and the uncontrollable bleeding begins. Laying there waiting on the doctor to give you a glimpse of hope. Instead, my lifeless baby is being pulled out of me and the doctor moves on to the next room as if nothing happened, as if 24 hours ago you weren't thinking of names or baby shower locations.

You know that cry, that ugly cry!? When your mouth is stretched wide open and you feel the cry deep down in your belly. The tears are falling, your nose is running. But there is no sound? Imagine that pain day in and day out. Feeling like a never-ending nightmare!

It's terrifying, embarrassing, yes embarrassing! As a woman I felt a certain way, after not being able to do what I was created to do... produce life!

Knowing this, I wondered what I did, didn't do or could have done to prevent this. Was it something I ate? Did I overdo it at work. Could it have been something in past, like some kind of karma that came to strike? A million little things going through my head as I laid on the hospital bed. My mom and husband sat silently in the room with me. I tried not to make eye contact with them, as we all felt the same thing. Grateful not to be alone yet, wanting to disappear from everyone's eye sight. The look of sorrow on the nurses faces as different ones entered to take vitals and or a shift change. "How are you doing?" to a Mother who just lost her baby is the most difficult question to answer. You can lie or just be real and say "How the hell do you think I feel" knowing it's not their fault so and brass reaction would be uncalled for. A weak "as good as can be expected" was the common reply.

The reality of it all didn't hit until I was at home alone. In the beginning people would call, text, etc. While I was pretending to be "ok". I had full blown meltdowns during the alone hours. Family and friends that would come by, I tried by best to not acknowledge the pain and depression I was battling. My answer to everything was "I'm ok" and making it believable behind fake smiles.

I really didn't know what to do. I had never felt these feelings before. Of course, loved one's transition throughout your life time. But this was a pain I had never experienced. The mental felt physical and vice versa. I had begun calling the 800 number for counseling. I went onsite to a counseling session. That was not to my liking at all. I felt as though the counselor was judging me. The questions she asked felt condescending.

I started talking to a Sister/friend Sha'Meca daily for prayer. She didn't know it at the time, but that was the only way I made it through. She wouldn't let me shut her out. She made herself available to and for me. Other time,s I remember showering my husband's back with tears as he slept. Falling asleep myself only to wake up and relive the same day over and over.

I was mad. I was angry. I was mad at myself. I was totally mad at God. How could God do this to me? Take my child from me? Why? Why me? When going to the doctor for a follow up, I felt a certain way about being around pregnant women and small children. There was a deep sadness that I can't explain. There is an emptiness that I was carrying around… why my child! Then having to explain what happened to those who wasn't aware on top of everything else was a hurdle within itself!

The loss of your child, the mental anguish, the emotional baggage. Finding out your body basically failed you. Fibroids grew faster than the baby and didn't allow any room for the baby to grow. Before being able to mentally and physically heal from the loss. Needing to have a Myomectomy to remove the 7 fibroids that ultimately suffocated your baby:

Having to be opened up again, and still with no baby to produce is another blow to the gut, both literally and figuratively. Each day I picked myself up and tried to do something to make this day better than the last.

There are people that expected me to get over it, not feel anything because MY baby wasn't full term. Or at a term the feasible for THEM to understand my pain. That was my baby! My baby, that gave me morning sickness, that I felt move and grow.

People suggested for me to just "have another one"… the audacity! I felt that was totally disrespectful. You can't replace children!

Miscarriage takes a toll on your life. Your marriage as well. As much as my husband attempted to be there. There is a feeling that he never fully understood what I was going through. Men grieve differently from women. They often times bond with the baby after it's born. I expected to physically see him breakdown as much as I was, to see him in tears daily. For him to open up and say something…anything that would compensate my feelings. I often times felt he had a lack of understanding for what I was going through.

There are other times I'd be upset, that he wasn't "visibly" broken by the loss of our child and I'd distance myself from him. Realizing now he grieved on his own, not needed to show me as proof. Your grief is yours and yours alone. You cannot expect others to feel the same as you do/did. Realizing we both were in our own recovery. There were times I'd cling to him just to hold me, with no words needing to be spoken.
Rebuilding my relationship with my spouse in the mist of rebuilding myself was taxing. Ultimately, we began making love again. I had to push past the thoughts and pain of what occurred over the last several weeks, mentally clearing your head, with hopes to "feel good" again is draining. I did not want my husband feeling unwanted, and I wanted to also feel desirable. Beyond the stretch marks and C-Section scars I wanted to feel beautiful and sexy again. It does happen, with time, patience and an understanding partner.

The fear of becoming pregnant again yet another hurdle. Wanting to have that feeling of life inside me again. The flutters, the excitement of finding out the gender. Yet, at the back of my mind I had haunting thoughts of losing another baby. Wondering if I could go through what I've just went through once again. Wondering if there was any damage done to the point where I wouldn't have any kids at all. I was in a constant battle with myself. What ifs come and go. Too try or not try again? Praying my body will be healthy enough to hold a baby full term.

Now, I understand that it was not my fault. The initial pain eases up. I remember the day my baby died, the date my baby was due. Every year is like I'm running track. At the date of the baby's death there's a hurdle I had to jump over, then the due date comes around... another hurdle! I cleared that until the next date comes around. Remembering that healing does not mean I've forgotten about my child. Not letting anyone make me feel celebrating my child's angelversary is insignificant.

For me there was hope at the end of the tunnel. 6 months later, another positive test! My "rainbow" baby boy (Ilijah) was on the way. Yes, I was terrified. I didn't want to do anything that would cause me to lose this baby. I was careful for all of those 9 months LOL. I literally felt like I was walking on eggshells until his arrival. When he arrived, I did everything short of wrapping him in bubble-wrap lol. 21 months after that, baby number 3 made his arrival. I was less stressed out with Ixavier. I felt powerful, like I can do this! And guess what? You can too!!

Coping:

First thing, above all else PRAY! The Most High God will supply and sustain your during the most terrifying times.

Secondly, begin speaking positivity over yourself, over your life. Write and remember daily Affirmations.
Here are a few that helped me:

I am Beautiful

I am capable of creating life

I am more than enough

Other people's thoughts do not define me

There is no one on earth like me

God created me divinely and unique

I am worthy

Today I will not stress over yesterday

I forgive myself

I love me

I am allowed to say no others and yes to myself

I am ok with not being ok!

I am grateful and blessed

I am a Survivor

I am a Virtuous Woman

Create a sacred space. Light candles, sit still, but do not dwell in unhappiness. You have to accept and be current in your feelings. This is the only way you'll overcome.

Utilize your resources! Talk it out with your partner. Talk to a friend you're not afraid of being transparent with. Seek the help of a Therapist. Write! Create a journal. Today I feel etc. The beauty of journaling is you can go back and read how far you've come. Wow, this time last year I was in a deep depression, fast forward to the present day, I am happy with life.

If you haven't experienced miscarriage yourself. But know someone who has. The best thing you can do is be a listening ear. Sometimes just the presence of someone else is comforting.

Baby Franklin

Loved with a Love beyond telling

Missed with a grief beyond all tears

7.7.11

Clear life's hurdles and run your race!

Regina Franklin Bio

Regina Anderson-Franklin is a Wife and Mother of 1 angel baby (Baby Franklin), two school age boys (Ilijah & Ixavier) and a Stepmom to 4 awesome bonus children. Regina is a freelance poetry writer. She's worked in Office Management for over 20 years.

She enjoys meditation, music and spending quality time with her family. She's taken courses at South Suburban College and obtained an EMT Certification. She is also a member of Daughter to Daughter Ministries. Regina is purpose driven and has a strong passion for helping others. Prayerfully her story can help many others clear life's their hurdles.

Chapter 12

And Then The Morning Comes...
Trust In The Rainbow

By Rev. Dr. Rene Minter

"Remain integral, teachable and steadfast in the faith while   enduring the storm as it is the prerequisite to your rainbow."

And then the Morning Comes Trust In The Rainbow

A rainbow is a bow or arc of prismatic colors appearing in the heavens opposite the sun and caused by the refraction and reflection of the sun's rays in drops of rain. In the book of Genesis, the rainbow represents the covenant of God for every living creature of every kind on the earth. "When I see the rainbow in the sky, I will always remember the promise that I made to every living creature. This is the symbol of the covenant that I've established between me and everything that lives on the earth." (Genesis 9:16-17). This covenant was established by God and given to Noah after the great storm of 40 days and nights that destroyed life as it was known. In both cases scientifically and biblically, the rainbow comes after a storm or disruption in the atmosphere. Rainbows are always precipitated by a storm.

The purpose of my portion of this anthology is address what happens when storms are prevalent in our lives. To borrow a popular colloquialism "into each life a little rain must fall." Undoubtably, we have all experienced cyclical highs and lows in which can cause short term disruption life outside our homeostasis, our status quo. For any woman who has gone into labor would clearly define that moment in time as crisis orientated. The labor process is disruptive for both the mother and the child, but it is of short duration and hopefully with a positive outcome of delivering a healthy baby. It is painful and disruptive (thank you Eve) but well worth the process. We can have both a positive and negative happening simultaneously.

I want to focus on something that is not spoken about much in the Christian Circles. Enduring despair, loss and descending to the point of depression and or anxiety. What happens when you are living for God and living by the rules, you are law abiding both spiritually and naturally and things array? What happens when you are in a position of leadership and healing within the community and you are the one in need? What happens when you have done all you know to do, fasted, prayed and attended church paid tithes and you find yourself sinking on every level as if you were standing on quicksand? What happens when you have recited every scripture encouraging faith and you feel it is no longer relatable? What happens when you're holding onto hope by a thread and the thread is unraveling? What happens when you can no longer fake it until you make it? You find yourself in a state where the projected image you want people to believe is even too difficult pull off. You find your reality unrecognizable. What happens when we live our lives with moral fortitude based on Godly principles and the storms keep coming? What is the purpose of the struggle and how do we navigate our way through? What happens when we talk the talk, but the walk become increasingly insurmountable? In my personal situation what did I have to be broken and was I broken for a cause? What happens when we who are steadfast in our faith find us in the trial of our faith. Despite all our best efforts including giving to the poor, attending church, praying, abiding by the tenants of the faith and you are thrown as major curb ball. Something so devasting that it brings to question all the good. What happens when you call on God about your depressing situation, you are descending in a whirlpool of depression finding the more you struggle to break free the greater the grasp is upon you. Your depressive situation now presents with the feeling of hopelessness which leads to depression and anxiety interchangeably? What happens when every scripture including God's desire for us to live a life of abundance is not your present reality? What do you do when you can't feel the hand of God on your life and much worse, you don't think he hears your prayer for relief or has forgotten about you? The word of God tells us to be anxious for nothing, yet very real situations of an adverse nature can cause anxiety. Anxiety is the unpleasant state of inner turmoil and the fear of the unknown. When struggling aimlessly in what appears to a hopeless situation the inner turmoil compounds and it presents with somatoform symptoms. Somatoform occurs when our bodies take on physical symptoms are the mind experiences i.e.: back and headaches, elevated blood pressure, and pain. The symptoms and the situation that lead to it are real. So, for these questions I inquired wisdom from God.

What happens when we are broken? Are broken for a cause?

 Without boast of personal character I know by the grace of God and the guidance of the Holy Spirit I have been an exceptionally good person. I stand out amongst others; I am a peculiar person. I have great compassion for humanity, willingness to demonstrate God's love and my kind spirit. Before I knew myself, God determined who I would be. Yes, I have had some detours and wrong turns, but I always return to my Godly design and love for humanity.

The point of the discussion is whatever the circumstance (you can fill in the blank) brokenness is brokenness. Whether it's the loss of a job, loss of a family member, divorce, social status it is a struggle, a spiral for which we often loose control of our homeostasis. If we are identified by the very thing that we have lost how do, we come to terms with our new reality?

I thought back over many of the horrific experiences I have endured, and I likened my life to that of a butterfly. The same butterfly that we see as a thing of great beauty goes thru an entire life of extreme struggle to get to that crowning moment of exquisite beauty. We see a butterfly and marvel at its beauty with the patterned markings and vibrant colors. I feel blessed when I encounter a butterfly and make note of the Godly artistry of this beautiful creature. Yes, we all see the beauty but seldom know the painstakingly struggle to achieve its' magnificence. We all know the butterfly originates as a wormy caterpillar and at some point, it emerges as the butterfly. Our human metamorphous is like the struggle of the butterfly. We "go through" as part of our metamorphous leading to goal achievement and a thing of beauty reflecting God's artistry upon us. We also go through life as that caterpillar attempting to survive against the odds, painfully growing, with our life sometimes turned upside down, bound by internal and external factors. If we can get through the process, we will become like the butterfly in all its beauty. We are designed by God for a purpose and to His glory.

I was born the unexpected second twin to a totally unprepared young married couple. My Mom had successfully delivered by sister and in the final portion of my sister's delivery was I discovered in the back of my Mom's womb. A much smaller and weaker baby who had to fight to survive in an incubator. I was a peculiar child growing up and never really fitting in with red hair and uniquely colored eyes. Although I looked different, I knew I was also internally different and often misunderstood. I was a remnant of sorts, but like that caterpillar, but God had a beautiful plan for my life.

I grew up in a neighborhood where the odds were against me. We were an African American family living in a Caucasian neighborhood during the height of the civil rights movement. Despite being told by teachers and students I was dirt, I did not belong there and of substandard intelligence. Despite being told I could never amount to anything I still managed to excel academically and never looked back. I knew education was the great equalized and once I understood that there was no stopping me for like the caterpillar to a butterfly, I would be a survivor. A bachelor's degree, Master's degree and Doctorate it was a struggle, but I would become a thing beautifully designed by God.

And then another storm, I had just returned from a mission's trip to Africa and had spent a large sum of money with the expectation that I would refund my bank account very easily with my salary. While in Africa donating food and materials to orphans which I did with an open hand as it was the work of the Lord. Who would know within one week of my return to work and my job as a Director no longer existed? I was totally broken but did not seek governmental assistance and the few who knew of my plight did nothing to help. I remember at my lowest boiling bones trying to make broth to drink. But I never gave up on God. I could not pay my bills, and everything fell behind and there was no hope in sight. I asked God to please send someone to help me, but it never happened. No one offered as much as a penny even out of pity for my situation. Broken but still holding on as I somehow still trying to conceive the premise that God had not forsaken me.

I had nothing but my trust and faith in God but where was He? Was God not seeing what has happening to His faithful servant? When would it end? I prayed, read my bible and found myself drawing closer to God. It was as though in the humiliation of the situation I gained humility and grew in the grace of God.

Every morning I began with prayer and prayed all day long. I prayed without ceasing, even while trying to rest I would wake up praying and yet life got harder. Gone were the days of going into the supermarket and buying whatever I wanted without concern for the cost. I remember in my former life, being annoyed by the customers in front of me on the supermarket checkout using the blue EBT card or the Women, Infant, Children (WIC) program. Instead, I know found myself looking at them with envy. Thankfully, as a social worker I had learned from my clients how to make meals stretch. I learned ramen noodles can be diversified many ways. I learned about couponing for survival not just to save a few pennies. I learned how to utilize and redeem points. I boiled bones to make broth and convinced myself I was full. I also understood why poor people don't eat well as good and nutritious food is beyond the scope of their financial means. Foods with high sodium and sugar are within their budget.

Things became so difficult for me that the things that were my norm were no longer part of my existence. Things like manicures, salon appointments, lunch with friends. I did not allow my grandchildren to visit my home as I had nothing to feed them. It broke my heart as every grandmother's desire to see their grandchildren as much as possible. Despite it all my family did not know my true situation as I was too ashamed to tell them. This storm or desert experience as I call it lasted for 8 weeks. I was broken but what was the cause?

I am blessed to have a part time psychotherapy practice for many years which I used to minimally sustain me. With whatever money I brought in it went immediately to try to pay something on one of the many bills. There was no extra anything. Yet I believed God for a miracle and wondered what the lesson was to be learned from this storm in my life. I knew I needed a miracle and that the miracle would outweigh the misery. I am so thankful for my desert experience as the 8 weeks in the wilderness.

I learned is pruning is part of the process. Just as with plants pruning is for my spiritual growth. The process of cutting off the things that were not relevant to my spirit needed to be disconnected before I move forward in Godly purpose. I learned that God will use whatever means He deems necessary to gain your attention. Perhaps the only way I could ascend spiritual was to descend in the natural. I had to be broken just like that caterpillar in order to emerge stronger and more dedicated to the things that really matter. In hindsight I believe my situation of loss and subsequent events were part of a greater plan.

My own insecurities cause me to ask, "I am enough?" My hemostasis is to be the supporter of the main character. But broken, now I am becoming center stage as a butterfly. As painful as the process for the caterpillar splitting its back to become that beautiful butterfly the process must take hold. Likewise, I had to be had to be broken by God.

The Humility Factor

I found the lower my circumstances became, the more connected I became with God. The natural hunger for physical nourishment was subsequently replaced by a hunger for God. We are creatures composed of mind body and spirit. During this desert experience it was the spirit portion of my being that sustained me when I thought my mind and body could go no further. It was as though my spirit spoke to God for me. There were times of awakening when my spirit was interceding when there were no more words. I could feel the very presence of God with me and I knew I was being broken for a purpose. Sometimes we are so caught up sublimating, going about the business of living and dealing with other's concerns that I was not addressing the spiritual deprivation of my own life. Oh yes, as I minister of the gospel, I knew the word of God, I knew how to pray for myself and others but clearly, I needed to go to a higher level. God needed to get my attention and break me to rebuild me. I was looking for that rainbow, but I had to first endure the storm. When it seemed, I could go no lower by societal expectation God was preparing me for elevation. Within a week I received a job offer for a major medical center paying more money than I could have imagined. I subsequently realized I needed to be broken in preparation for that moment.

I thought I could never be enough that; my insecurity was greater in my mind than my ability. Even when I looked at all I have done in my life I was still selling myself short and wanting to stay in the comfort zone of the self-imposed cocoon. What God has shown me is my role of support and nurturance will always be there as its who I am. God uses me mightily, but now with greater spiritual insight. I was broken for a purpose. This writer of the past saw herself as the captain of my own ship, that I had some say in my destiny. My sixty-day journey through the dessert has enabled the comprehension that I am just a vessel, a mound of clay to be used by God who orchestrates His will in my life. I'm a minister who by the grace of God treats humanity through my humility, with dignity and respect. I am a Christian woman who speaks openly about loss, depression and mental illness in the Christian community. I have been used to debunk the myths and stereotypes of shame. I teach Clergy globally and love that God can use me mightily and the integration of support and education to leadership. I AM ENOUGH thanking you Lord.

The Rest Factor

In prayer I asked the Lord, why I had to go through this and what was I to learn. In my spirit received REST. REST? If there was anything that did not happen it was rest as my days were filled with anxiety and night were never an escape from the day time misery. Rest but I'm broken Lord. Rest?

In the sweetness of the Lord I received this:

R …. Rely on God for restoration

E…. Establish the time and the faith for restoration

S…...Stop worrying as it opposes faith

T…. Trust God in the restorative process.

We are all familiar with the footprints story. When there was only one set of footprints it was God who carried the writer. The carrying during what seems like impossible times in the dessert is grace. Grace; the unmerited favor of God to complete what seems impossible or insurmountable. So, when stuck, don't abort the dream, find support network, pray and let grace lead your way. In the process we must understand that poverty, hunger, depression and anxiety exist in the church. There is no shame in seeking help when needed. Trust the process. God has provided us with what we need to get us through including receiving help from the right people.

Remain Teachable

I have learned that God can use us for His purpose and if we are in a useable state due to spiritual arrested development we may need to be broken. Sometime, as in my case, there needed to be the process of descending to ascend. It was necessary for me to be relieved of the some of the things that I once valued as critical elements of my existence to gain spiritual insight of what was critical to my spirit. It was necessary for me to surrender my will and let God's will take control. I am learning now having endured so many storms that they are all teachable moments that provide immeasurable insight for practical application in our service to mankind.

I am a Christian Based Psychotherapist who lives in a state of gratitude for the opportunities that have been afforded me. My attitude of gratitude promotes a Godly altitude. I remain teachable and no longer look at obstacles the same way. I now value them now as growth potential. Each obstacle and challenge represent another stage of my metamorphosis. I believe God designs us all for a purpose as stated in Jeremiah 29:11

"For I know the plans I have for you, declared the Lord, plans to prosper you and not harm you, plans to give you hope for the future."

I serve an awesome God who has a plan for our lives. There is nothing that says will be no struggles, but we do have the assurance God is omnipresent, He cares about us and wants us to live a life of abundance. Even Job who suffered beyond anything we could imagine recovered double what he lost.

While in that caterpillar stage our lives are turned upside down and we are bound hold fast to God and His promises. I thank God for my caterpillar to butterfly experiences which remain cyclical in my life.

There are moments when I am placed in a cocoon for Godly adjustment. There are times when I'm in the valley surrounded by challenges and struggles but God has never forsaken me, and like the caterpillar, once the problem is released, the butterfly emerges. I am that unexpected child who was

127

survived against the odds, equalized by education, overcome childhood prejudice, divorce and yes, the struggle was painful, but the product is a thing of Godly beauty. So, whether I am working with addicts, the mentally or terminally ill, treating psychiatric patients, providing hope for the hopeless, housing for the homeless, holding the hand of someone transitioning from life to their eternity or in ministry in Africa find myself thankful to be used in God's service.

"Lord, help me to remember as You prepare me to soar like the butterfly that it is You who provides the wind beneath my wings. I remain humble and grateful in spirit while there is a concurrent process of elevation of altitude. I am grateful for caterpillar to butterfly experiences and thankful that God is with me always in the process."

We are expected to continue to learn and grow throughout our lifespan. Chronologically at the age of 21 we are considered adults. Although fully grown by appearance it does not mean we he met all the developmental milestones. If we did not successfully complete al developmental milestone, we are considered to have arrested development. For some, it becomes a task to attempt to amend the issues and continue growing. I believe the same is true in our spiritual walk; we need to continue growing. It took 60 days in the dessert broken and striped of everything for me to be restored by with new and improved parts.

My Heart

A heart desiring to live and express the love of God like never before and at a much higher level. A heart for the lost and the suffering. A heart of flesh filled with charity and compassion; a desire to do the will of God.

My Mind

A mind to think consistently about the blessings and what can I do to be used by God each day. A heart to want to minister and help those in need. A mind to seek wisdom and to remain in a state of humility always remaining grateful.

My Ears

Two ears to hear God in my prayers and in reading His word. Ears to hear what needs to be heard. Ears that are formulated hear the needs of those in pain and suffering.

My Eyes

Two eyes to see the work of God, my blessings large and small. Eyes to recognize pain and to be part of the healing process.

I am that caterpillar who struggled through may storms to become a butterfly and found my rainbow. I now realize the rainbow cannot appear without the storm. As difficult as it may sound the 60 days in the desert has taught me to endure the storm to get to the rainbow. I have learned the value of the REST principle providing trust in God and allowing the restorative process to take hold. Yes, weeping may endure for the night and maybe even 60 nights but then the morning comes.

Rev. Dr. Rene Minter Bio

Rev. Dr. Rene Minter is a Christian Based Psychotherapist in private practice in New York. She has been and is the Director of non-for-profit management. She is a social worker by profession with a master's degree in Clinical Social Work. She possesses a Doctorate in Ministry and is a certified chaplain. She her the call to ministry as a young child and was ordained in 2015. She is devoted to the ministry of missions globally. She provides charitable support to women and children in Africa. She has held NGO responsibility with the United Nations. She is an Author, Blogger, Podcaster, Motivational Speaker, Humanitarian.

In her spare time, she enjoys being Meamawh to her four grandchildren children.

Chapter 13

Boom, Click & Dial Tone God Carried Me
"Working the Win Within"

By Shay Lewis Sisco

"Influenced by experience, Inspired by God"

Boom, Click & Dial Tone
God Carried Me
"Working the Win Within"

Lost, empty and helpless she stood without any guidance or a sense of direction. Every night she falls to sleep, what she expected to be peace felt more like torture while having nightmares before she was able to identify that the message behind her dreams. Growing up in a single parent household with other siblings made her ability to identify who she really was very difficult considering the factors that aligned the structure of the home. She was the baby girl, middle child of 3. She was me!

There are so many parts of my childhood, I can recall clearly while others are very faint. Phone rings, I panic, afraid to answer it so after hesitation but decides to answer. In a whisper, I say hello. Boom, click and then dial tone; eernkk, eernkk, eernkkk. My mind begins to wonder, "Who was that? what was that about and why was this happening to me?" This was definitely one of the defining moments in my life; as this event played over time and time again in my mind. Not really understanding the phone call or the message that could have come from the call, but it definitely woke me up. These phone calls turned into dreams that made it difficult to sleep at night so my mind believed that if I went to sleep during the day around everyone else then it would stop. Boom, click and dial tone; eernkk, eernkk. The boom felt like a painful crush; the click felt like rejection, and the dial tone felt like emptiness. This happened so many times that sometimes, I couldn't tell you if I was actually dreaming or if it was my reality.

However, it didn't stop until years later. My lack of understanding caused me to lose hope within myself so I began gravitating to anything and anyone who was willing to accept me. There were many times when I needed people and no one was there. When I would call, all I would get was Boom, Click and the dial tone. Growing up without my father in my life, mother that was not home often because she worked all the time, being teased because of my weight, because my father was not around led to me suffering greatly with abandonment issues. While mom worked, most times my siblings and I watched ourselves. Mom would call home to check on us, every break and she would want to speak to all of us so she knew we were all in the house. One day she called home, my sister answered the phone, my brother was still outside so she sent me after him while she stalled mom on the phone telling her that we were getting showers; I ran outside through the path to get my little brother only to for some man to grab me up and rapped me. I was *terrifieddd*! Now, violated by a complete stranger, feeling like it was my fault and still in complete disbelief. I sat in the tub, face in a towel, screaming, sobbing and out of touch with myself. I didn't know what to do, I couldn't tell my mom because I had no business being outside and feared that she would blame me for what had happened to me. So, this time while mom was actually calling to check on us and my sister answered her call. I was actually calling her but again all I got was boom, click and the dial tone.

This shifted me in so many ways that I couldn't even put my emotions into words. So, I chose to hide between or behind other people so that I wasn't seen to ditch the embarrassment of who people perceived me to be and what I looked like. These things cause me to become disgusted with myself. While hiding between and behind others, I suppressed my thoughts and feelings because I lost sight of who I was. I mean when I would speak it was either a joke or people didn't take me seriously. While going through these times I was very emotional, passive and easily offended leaving me heartbroken and alone all over again. Feeling the boom, click and dial tone once again.

After suffering great heartaches at the hands of those very people I hid between and behind because when they finally realized that I was in between or behind them; the response from them made me feel like they were uneasy about my presence thinking that I was around only to get what I could from them. What they could NOT identify was all I was looking for was someone to love me for me, someone to accept me without talking about my weight or my lack thereof but just someone who would identify my potential to have patience with me through my process. This all sounds complicated and a bit much for someone else who is just as lost as I was. Eventually, I understood I couldn't hide or between my friends or those family members that wanted to deal with me for that moment. One of the worst feelings in the world is being born into a family that you feel as if you were never accepted. Outcasted and let down by the ones you hold dear to your heart is worse than experiencing that heart from a stranger. This was difficult because I had a family with in my very first church Mt. Moriah Assembly of Faith. My best-friend and the church followed the call of God to move the church to Aberdeen, Maryland. This was challenging for me because my only outlet and the one friend that I felt genuinely loved and cared for me was now leaving me. While I had no other choice to understand, again all I had replay in my head was the boom, click and dial tone

After my church family moved, I still was eager to stay connected to God, so I joined another ministry and was loved on by each person in the church. I enjoyed the services and appreciated the love but was hungry for more, so I was led to stop into a bible study being taught by my former Pastor who I found out the since evening was my family. I was totally blown by the teaching and eager to learn more, I went back Sunday for service and attended a few more bible studies until I eventually joined. A few months after joining, Pastor was able to see God's hand upon my life, he taught me more about the Holy Spirit which I appreciated because it helped me to understand the dreams and phone calls that I never got clarification about from years ago. My spiritual vision became real and I started operating in the spirit as if I had never experienced before. I went forth, feeling useful and appreciated for a while. People calling and depending on me for prayer and encouragement. Pouring out to not having no one pour back in, left me empty. Trying to reach out for someone but didn't know who I could reach for without being judged or taken for granted. So, I felt that I lost touch again, felt alone and outcast again so I walked away. So here we go again; boom, click and dial tone. I went to my Pastor gave him back the license to minister. Completely puzzled with tears in his eyes, he asked was everything ok and of course I lied. Gave him the license and walked out of the church. All of these efforts caused me to have low self-esteem, lack of confidence while dealing with fear of rejection. I found myself living a life to please people while silently suffering.

Since I felt there was no place for me in the church, with my friends or family, I resorted to love in the form of a man that gave me attention and said I was beautiful. What I did not realize was the responsibility that came with a relationship or a family. I had to learn quick and throughout the process the transition wasn't easy, nor do it feel well but I humbled myself and did it. Going through so much in the house with my mom because I started to feel like I had more responsibility that I thought I should have for years. Times where my mom would wake me up out my sleep when she got off of work at 2:00 am because I didn't complete my chores and clean the way she would. I remember my mom waking me up one night when she got off of work because I had cleaned the bathroom but since it was cleaned the way she would have cleaned it so with great attitude I got up not fussing and went into the bathroom to start cleaning it. Half way still asleep, moving slow because I was aggravated that she was making me do it all over again, so she cracked me on my hands with the broom. That was the straw for me, something stood up in me and I told her I didn't want to live with her anymore. I grabbed the phone and called the cops, begged them to take me out of her house. Unfortunately, the cops said that I wasn't old enough for emancipation and that I wasn't living in conditions that warrant for them to remove me from the house. I felt completed defeated and angry! So, of course I had to do something and something quick.

The next day I woke up with a change mindset that I wasn't going to be pushed around any longer. I had the enough is enough mindset! So, when I got to school I just began to watch and eagerly look at the clock for the day to be over because I was on a mission. What I failed to mention early was that the relationship that I found in the man that took interest in me was that he was older and stable. He had his own apartment, car and a decent job. So after school I knew I was going to his house to spend time with him. Still not understanding the dynamics of a relationship but I knew that I couldn't continue feeling like I was in my mom's house. Him and I started making plans to make our relationship official. I knew that our relationship was about to be taken to the next level so I start making preparations in my mind on how I was going to make this situation work. My mom and stepdad went out a few weeks after I called the cops, begging them to take me out of her house and brought me my first car. Although, I had to make the payment, the gesture was nice. So now with a car, a made-up mind that my boyfriend and I was making it official. Chilllleeee, you couldn't tell me nothing now. Once I got home, I knew I had chores and I completed them, I started mumbling under my breath when my mom would ask me to do things, I just started to not care anymore because my plan was set and I just knew this plan was going to be the one to change my life for the better. My attitude created barriers that caused additional separation between me and my mother.

At this point of my life, I truly believed that at this point my mom felt that I was above myself and I honestly didn't care because I was sick of not being heard, accepting anything someone threw my way because they were comfortable with it. I felt as if my kindness had for the last time been taking for my weakness. It was like a bad case of mistaken identity. The pain, the backlash, heartaches and rejection didn't belong to me any longer. So, I proceeded to make a move on the plans I had made with my boyfriend. At this point, I am a senior in high school, working at Burger King, now about to move in with my boyfriend. After moving in with my boyfriend, I felt like this was the fresh start I needed, no nagging, no chores, no being woke up at night to do chores over and no one to answer too. Yup, you guess it. I forced myself into adulthood because I felt that I had already had the responsibilities while living at home with my mom. However, after a month, things started to change in my relationship; the man so loving and respectful had become very irritable and snappy lately. I didn't understand it, all of a sudden there were arguments over nothing. So, I felt like it, I mean I was going to school, working a job and still coming home to cook, clean and now that we had become intimate, maintaining his happiness the best I knew how. So here I am with the thoughts that life was about to be perfect, hoping and wishing this relationship/love thing was going to be my happy ever after story. So much for that! The happily after ever, turned into another disappointment and a whole different level of hurt. The first time in a while that I felt like I belonged calling for him and all I got was boom, click and the dial tone. I was not even a month away from graduating high school for me to find out that I was pregnant! Yup, pregnant. What most consider to be news to celebrate, sang to me as news for another death sentence.

My thoughts went from "How could this be happening to me? Why now? I can't believe I did this to myself too well at least I will have someone to truly love me for me. I know I can do this. I mean although this isn't the life I dreamed about but I have to deal with my consequences. I had not only separated myself from my family but also my friends. However, when in doubt I knew I could call on my two besties so that's what I did. After I spoke to them and told them I was pregnant, the only thoughts that penetrated my mind was now they really ain't gonna like me. However, those were the two that I found to be the most supportive. The arguments continued between my boyfriend and I and my attitude got worse with each passing day. I made the decision to save myself and the one person I didn't want to run back too, I had no other choice but to turn too. Yup, my mom! I had no one else to help me pick up the pieces and as bad as it hurt me to be going back to her. As a mom, I am sure she wanted to say something like "you're not as grown as you thought you were, huh" but she didn't. However, once I moved back home, her actions made me feel everything she did not say. Maybe it wasn't her actions, just maybe it was in my mind, so I thought. With each passing month, I was slowly losing myself again!

I went with the motions for months until after graduation. I found it difficult to continue to work because I was always so sick. I maintained myself the best I could without asking anyone for anything because I didn't want to be a burden on anyone especially now carrying a child. That was a bit much to ask someone to help with. So, I play the background again and moved silently trying to hide. I ended up making friends with an older lady who was very nice to me, opening up her home, sharing her kids with me and I felt comfortable because it was like she let me be me. She was very accepting to my thoughts, ideas and opinions. Although, my mom didn't care for the friendship, I refused to let my mom know where I was going when I left the house. So, one night I had went to sleep early and woke up bored, so I decided to call her. We were on the phone talking and then I heard one of the kids say they were hungry. She soon said, girl let me call you back. Shortly after she called back and said I just ordered some food from Denny's do you mind taking me to pick it up. Without hesitation I said, give me a minute, I will be right there. Picked her and we headed straight to Denny's to pick up the food. She went in and I sat in the car in front of the restaurant. While I thought she would be in and out this took a lot longer than I anticipated and my pregnant-blatter was on full, so I tried to wait it out but couldn't. So, I left the car running, to go inside to go use the restroom, only for me to come out and she was still waiting on her food to step outside to find that someone had stolen my car! My life was breaking again, all I could think was here I go again. Of course, my mom flipped out, especially when she found out that I had taken the friend that she didn't want me hanging out anywhere. A few hours went by, my mom received a called they had found the car but didn't catch the thief. Car goes in the shop now I am sitting home pregnant, looking crazy. While I felt horrible, I felt like this was my time to reconnect myself to God because I knew it was nobody but him that carried me through all this I had went through. After feeling reassured that God's covering was surrounding and carrying me, I felt ready to jump back in. The sickness from my pregnancy started to ease up. So I went looking for another job, dressing back up, no longer laying around and just now starting to feel like myself. So now here I am almost 5 months pregnant going in for my appointment to check on the baby. The doctor inquires if I would like to get the AFP testing done, at the appointment. Of course, not knowing what it was I asked, what is the test for? The doctor replied that the test will detect any abnormalities in your pregnancy.

A few weeks later the test results came back and to my surprise I receive a call that the results were abnormal. My OBGYN scheduled a specialist to come from Annapolis to Salisbury Maryland to complete a 3D/4D sonogram to check on the baby. I will never forget telling my child's father that this was an appointment he should have made. He made up every excuse as to why he couldn't take off to go. Needless to say, I drove myself to the appointment only to find out that my son had passed. I assured the doctor that I just felt the baby kick on my way to the appointment and he affirmed, "No Ms. Lewis, that could have been a flutter" but, he confirmed again my baby had passed. I gazed at the Specialist with a look of confusion and questioned, what happens now? His reply was you should contact your OBGYN. Back feeling hopeless and confused again. I don't know what to do or where to go but as soon as I walked out the office I got sick and throw up everywhere. "Urghhh", I screamed, got in my car and proceeded down the highway. Here feeling the boom- crashing pain, click- rejection and dial tone-empty; the one thing, only thing that I believed would never leave me, judge me and genuinely love me has been snatched from me.

The minute I got in my car, I got sick again but this time all over myself almost running off the road. I was angry, hurt, and unsure what to do next. Days had gone by and I was still pregnant with the knowledge that I was carrying a deceased baby in me. After a week, of literally hell on earth, my aunt went to the hospital and raised sand! I mean she went completely off, at this time my mom was establishing her relationship with God and felt that prayer could do more than anything else. Today, I stand with the understanding that faith alone is dead. The scripture James 2:26 confirms that "Faith without works is dead". So, although she was praying to God, physically, mentally and emotionally I was losing it. Needless, to say after my aunt carried on the doctors, started to move quickly to start the induction process. After being in labor 12 hours and 20 minutes, I gave birth to my week-old deceased son. I named him Ja'Quan Tyrone Lewis. My mom ended up coming to the hospital to provide support, I reached out to my son's father to see if he was going to come over to the hospital. His response was "I am out of town, looking for an outfit to wear to the funeral". In my mind, I wanted to flip but I was so drained by the entire birthing process, seeing my son and then having to remain on the hospital floor where I cried to the cry of the other babies.

This was the greatest hardship that I had ever experienced and the life changing event that sent me back to that pit. Feeling like maybe it is me, nothing will work for me. If I touch it or get involved it will go sour and turn for the worst. So I went into this depression and at the young age of 18, found myself drowning my sorrows in a liquor bottle. Underage drinking, but I was so deep in my depression that it didn't matter how old I was or that I wasn't supposed to be drinking. I enjoyed the feeling of feeling free although I still dealt with the pain of losing the one thing I thought would bring me joy, that would love and accept me for me. I turned away from God, lost myself again. However, my former Pastor and church family (St. John's Holiness Church) still loved on me. They raised all the money that was needed to bury my son. While the support and love were given, the pain never seemed to go away. E&J (my drink of choice, music and work was my escape from the pain, so I thought for 2 years. I started having the dreams again, now terrified to answer the phone, I just let it ring. I was tired of hearing boom, click and dial tone. I was sick of crashing painful feelings of rejection and emptiness.

Shortly, after realizing my success couldn't be gain standing between or behind the crowd of people that I was associated with. As well as acknowledging that success wouldn't be found in the alcohol, I stepped back into the habit of prayer. Once I started to pray and attend church again I begin feeling a little better, but I was not stable enough to give up alcohol completely. So, the drinking slowed down, I started to be accepting to friendships again but not fully giving myself out of fear that something horrible would happen or I would end up hurt. I kept on going to church and the more I went the better I felt. My former pastor as well as other ministers would minister to me about the call that was on my life and although I knew I was different. I felt as if I failed in the ministry because I turned my back on God. However, what I didn't realize was that although I went through so much, turned my back on God even left him and walked away. He never turned his back on me. He allowed me to see who I was called to be, he raised me up again to believe in myself once again. I came out of hiding and accepted the process required my participation. I sought out counseling. My cousin, LeeLee texted me on Easter Sunday out the blue in 2009; she invited me over and that night I remember staying until like 3am. We talked, I cried, she encouraged me, and I couldn't wait to talk to her again. She gave me hope! Years went by and LeeLee schooled me on so much but more importantly seeing the value in myself. This was one of the first times I felt that when I called someone was actually on the other end.

After being told I couldn't carry children full term, today I stand a proud wife and mother of 4. Standing in my truth, working the win within me. I realized from all that I had experienced that even when I felt as if I was losing, it was all a part of the WIN that God was working to manifest today to bless someone else on their journey. Now, hearing the ringing of the phone; I answer without hesitation because the call is different. I have submitted my will and answered the spiritual call. NO longer am I hearing the boom, click and dial tone. I asked that you take inventory to identify what is your boom, click and dial tone? Acknowledge it, don't run from it. Breaking the Code of Silence starts with you NOW. My encouragement to you reading this is remember no matter how hard it gets, remember his word in the scripture, Numbers 23:19, "God is not a man that he should lie; neither the son of man, that he should repent: hath he said, and shall he not do it? or hath he spoken, and shall he not make it good"? What I realized in all this was that

I couldn't ride off the success or accomplishments of others. The call I kept seeking someone to answer for me, GOD was waiting on me to answer from him. I had to put in the work, have patience and trust that the same way God carried me through all that he brought me through without losing my mind. He will continue to do just what Numbers 23:19 promised me. I no longer stand behind or between the people that I hang with, I have learned that the greatest WIN in life is when you can "Work the Win Within".

Today, I am a faithful member at Living by Truth Ministries under the leadership of Pastor Lamont and Mia Jackson. I am honored to have a great husband, 4 beautiful children, amazing friends and family (Matt 12:49-50). Realizing an I had to leave I must stand on my own, while I have to work out my own soul salvation, this journey is one that I must share with others. All of these experiences, has given me the courage to carry out the vision God entrust me with so I stand humbly as the visionary and CEO of WOW (Wisdom Optimizes Winning) Inspired which is an organization that educates, serves and supports aspiring leaders to re-energize, revive and ignite their passion to walk into their purpose. Known as "ShaySpeaks", here to Inspire the Influencer in YOU. Follow our social media outlet @iamshayspeaks on FB, IG and YouTube. Pictured below was captured by: Photographer Myra Sisco! This is what living the WOW Inspired life looks like for me now in 2019.

Shay Lewis Sisco Bio

Shavonte "Shay" Lewis-Sisco also known as ShaySpeaks is the visionary and CEO of WOW Inspired: an organization that educates, serves and supports aspiring leaders and career professionals to re-energize, revive and ignite their passions to "walk in their purpose" through strategic planning, coaching, speaking engagements and writing projects.

More than the Founder and CEO of WOW Inspired, Shay is a Servant Leader, Public Speaker, Life and Career Advocate with a welcoming smile and a grassroots approach that exemplifies her small town upbringing on the Eastern Shore of Maryland, where she suffered through a failed marriage, loss of a child at 18, depression, and the rejection of those who she once valued as friends and members of her family all before the age of 25. It was in this darkness that the sparks began to ignite the fire within Mrs. Lewis-Sisco and light the path towards her life's true calling. Shay has a unique passion for helping others, building community and engaging those who have been left behind or have felt that they are not good enough because they have been rejected so many times. Through her personal struggles, Shay learned the importance of having an advocate, whether though therapy or the counsel of community faith-based leaders. Shay uses social media platforms such as Facebook, You Tube, and Instagram to spread inspirational messages, information, and sage advice to those who view and follow her. "I strongly believe that there is something greater in each of us and feel purposed to inspire others to bring the greater you out of you."

Chapter 14

Moving Forward: 12 Hours Later

By Sherie Billingslea

Moving Forward: 12 Hours Later

I had no idea that this would be our last meal together, the last time I'd hug him or tease him about being a Dallas Cowboy fan and him declining my many attempts to convert him over to becoming a Washington Redskins fan.

It's been more than ten months since my Bishop, my mentor, my friend and my father-in-law transitioned to sleeping in peace forever. Like many I thought he'd live forever or at least to a one hundred (100) years old. He was so wise. He was a honest man, a great husband, a great dad, a great leader and he had a great sense of humor to my surprise. He was an old school somewhat traditional man, a bishop, a husband, a dad, a granddaddy, a friend, a brother and so much more.

It was the day before Thanksgiving 2017 I had called my in-laws house, to talk to my mother in-law (note I am divorced but, I still refer to my in-laws as "in-laws", because they are awesome people) to see how she was doing and if she needed me to grab anything for the next day: Thanksgiving dinner.

My father in law answered and said, "you just missed her, she's out running errands for tomorrow." I smiled, nodded my head and said "ok". As I was about to say, "tell her I called", he sparked up a conversation with me, that was starting to happen more often when I call to talk to my mother in law and she wasn't home or had to call me back.

Any way, we spent at least 30 minutes talking about how much Khloe my daughter, his granddaughter had grown, how smart she is, and he shared with me some thoughts he had about Khloe's future. As he was a former educator for more than 20 years he understood the importance of an education and how some students fell through the cracks because they weren't labeled with any disorders or had behavior issues.

He shared with me how in the coming months he would have more time and would love to spend some of that time with Khloe helping her with home-work, enhancing her analytical and problem-solving skills and just spend more time with her. In the midst of the conversation he brought up the pre-vious year Thanksgiving dinner and he noticed I wasn't in attendance. That year my ex-husband remarried and even though we all were in a good space, being parents and navigating our blended family. I didn't want to feel awk-ward, so I opt-out for my own personal reasons.

My father in law said "you know your family too and I hope to see you tomorrow. Are you coming tomorrow?" I smiled because I did know that, my in-laws and the extended family remain consistent with me from the time I met them at the age of 19 years old to the current day. This family chose to love me no matter what, even when they didn't have to, even after the divorce they remained the same. (Hmm, that was a journey for me all by itself) I said, "yes I'll be there."

After that we chatted a lil while longer and before we hung he said, "Imma see you tomorrow, right?" I said "yes, dad you'll see me tomorrow", we said our "alrights" and hung up. If I knew that would have been our last phone conversation, we would have talked until my cell phone battery died. I would have thanked him again for being such an awesome person, an awesome granddad, a great mentor, a friend and a phenomenal father in law. I would have shared with him, how much his granddaughter admired him, how she talked about him constantly and how I love him forever to the stars and back.

It reminds me of how much the present is really a gift and even though I didn't get the chance that day to say it, I had told him that numerous of times before, so the conversation we had then was a gift, the present moment of us talking, laughing, reflecting and talking about the future would replay over and over in mind. I smile to myself, gathered my belongings and my "get it done" list to complete the tasks I listed for the day. Not knowing the next 12-24 hours would drastically change my life and my connection to one of my favorite holidays: Thanksgiving.

We all gathered at my uncle in laws house for Thanksgiving dinner. EVERY-ONE was there, we greeted each other, helped with last minutes things, laughed and then blessed the food. After the blessing, some of us retreated to different areas of the house, majority of us including myself, my cousin in laws, my in-laws and a few long-time family friends sat at the table to enjoy our meal and watch the Washington Redskins vs. Dallas Cowboys game, a family tradition and with football comes talking trash.

We teased my father-in-law as he was the only Cowboys fan at the table. We enjoyed our meal, continued to laugh and talk about a variety of things from politics to investing money to upgrading the church where he was the Bishop. As the evening unwind, we started to clean up and pack up our to-go plates. My father-in-law walked into the living room and sat down in a lounge chair, I got caught a glimpse of him looking at my brother-in-law obituary that sat on the mantle. My brother-in-law had passed away that summer, I continued to help in the kitchen and then I heard him say "Sherie babe, can you get me a bottle of water?" "Yes", I replied, and I gave him a bottle of water "thank you", no problem Da and I went back into the kitchen.

A few moments later, my mother in law came to me to share that Da was feeling good and they were about to leave. Ok momma, he probably ate too much. We packed up our bags, hugged and kissed each other and went our separate ways.

I drove home not thinking too much of what my mother in law said I was thinking about the great evening we had and how we joked about getting up tomorrow to go to Black Friday, we never had done that before. I was excited about tomorrow, I went to bed full, happy, and at ease. I woke up the next morning, refreshed and excited. I called my mother in law and jokily said, "Are you ready to fight these people for a 52 inch TV." There was no laughter coming from the other end of the phone, "daddy wasn't feeling well last night, can you come to the hospital daughter?"

My heart beat increase, the bridge of my nose started to throb, then the throbbing made its way up to my temples, around my head, and down my neck. The fear and the stress sat on my shoulders like concrete blocks. Next thing I knew I was at the hospital, standing at the foot of his bed in shock. "Who the hell is this"?! I said to myself in a state of shock, this is not the man I saw last night, ate with and laughed with. I stood silently with my thoughts not wanting to add on to the stress, this was not the man I had seen 12 hours ago.

I felt like I was in the twilight zone or having some weird outer body experience, as I greeted my brother in law, my sister in law, my aunt in law and we all turned around as the nurse greeted us and began to tell us the next steps. I couldn't hear anything, her mouth was moving, I could see the expressions on everyone's face and all I kept thinking was "what"? Then I heard my brother in law say, "we'll get back to you." His voice snapped me back to reality and I blurted out "they do what they have to do and, in the meantime,, we goin pray." That's what we did, we held hands, bowed our heads and prayed.

You know the saying "what's understood, doesn't need to be said", we all felt the same way, I could feel it and we all chose not to say anything, for this was not the time. "For faith is the substance of things hoped for, the evidence of things not seen." I said that scripture to myself, gave everyone a hug and started to walk to the parking garage to my car, to drive home. As I walked through the hospital double doors to the elevator, I told myself "he'll bounce back like always and he'll have a mean testimony to share with the congregation, how he picked up his bed and walked in Jesus Christ name."

The following months my faith was tested and challenged, I start out strong praying without ceasing, choosing to not accept what was being shared with me, what natural eyes witness during my visits. I meditate, I prayed, I consecrated, I spoke words of life over the situation, but as the days turned to weeks and the weeks turned to months. I became weary, I began to cry, I began to isolate myself, sleep less and drink more. Right before bed, I would sit on my couch, staring at my electric fireplace with my wine glass, my wine, and my tears.

I had visited him numerous of times and focused on any signs of hope, restoration, and recovery. I celebrated the small victories and told myself he is going to have a powerful testimony. During all of this some parts of my life was thriving, and other parts was a complete MESS. I had learned that my grandmother was in the hospital after falling in her apartment and no one being able to contact her for two days. My uncle arrived at her apartment to find her on her floor, my dad had reached out to my sisters and I, we all rode together to see our grandmother. I was relieved to see her, her leg was swollen but she was ok, still spunky, cracking jokes, making everyone laugh and feel good.

You know the saying "God doesn't put more on you than you can bear." I thought to myself, he must think I am a bear and that I can bear a lot. On the outside it appeared that way, but on the inside, I was breaking down. I was losing my grip, losing hope, losing faith, and losing focusing. So, the only thing I felt like I had a grip on was a nice cold beer or a nice glass of wine, that would turn into drinking a six-pack or a bottle of wine alone, depending on how sorry I felt for myself. I continued this cycle, I would work, stop at the store, shower, sit on my couch, wake up looking like dog poop, force myself to work and repeat.

I would visit my father-in-law, when allowed, some days it was best that I stay home and pray. So, when I could visit him, I would play him songs from one of his favorite singers Anita Baker. I would talk to him and sit across his bed just so he felt that he was not alone. Sometimes I would go straight home or visit my mother in law, sit, and chat with her for hours.

She is my Ruth and I am her Naomi, my life was like a tornado from work to hospital visits to trying to be a present mom, tutoring sessions, cleaning the house, going to the grocery store and more. I had to press myself to do the normal things. I kept myself busy and I kept my faith, during this time I exercised my faith like none other. I prayed, I mediated, I exercised, and life kept going.

It was a beautiful spring day, I was on my way to work jamming to the radio, my direct deposit had hit my account. I was in a good mood. My phone rang, I answered,"Hello?" "Hey, Sherie" the male voice on the other end of my line, I knew his voice. The way he said my name sent chills down my spine. "Hey, good morning" "hey, da left this morning" was what he said. I had to pull over on the shoulder, I was silent, the bright blue sky turned gray to me and a part of my heart was snatched out of my chest and tossed on the beltway as many cars and trucks drove over it. "Hello, hello, Sherie you heard me?" "Yes, I am driving, I'll call you when I am safe." "Ok" he said.

I called my supervisor who had been well aware of what I was going through, she answered so chipper "Hey! Ms. Billingslea" I could feel her smile and that's when I broke down. I cried, I told her, he was gone! I told her how tired I'd been these last few months, forcing a smile on my face when all I wanted to do was cry. I told her I am not as strong as I appear. I am tired, I am hurt, he was my person, my mentor, my friend, my dad, he was more than an in-law, more than a Bishop to me and now he is GONE!

He had seen my highs, my lows, my losses, my victories and he remained the same. He was one of the realest n****s I knew, and I meant that with as much respect as possible. He never judged me, he never changed on me, he was honest, he was respectful, he carried himself with excellence. He was able to "put me in my place" from a place of love, he was able to correct me and build me up at the same time.

I hung up with my supervisor and drove home, I sat in my parking lot pissed! Then my phone rang hang and it was my mother in law, I could hear the pain, the anguish, the sadness in her voice. She lost her best friend, the love of her life, the devoted father of her children, her confidant for more than 50 years. I sat in my car, in my parking lot in a daze.

It was a beautiful ceremony, lots of things were said about him that we all knew, it felt so surreal. We buried dad, he received his flag and my mother in law would eventually receive a letter from the current President of the United States of America expressing his condolences and gratitude for my father in law services to the USA.

As time passed I became angry and resentful towards God, I couldn't understand why he would take my father in law, a man that was impacting the community and leaving other scumbags here to run a munk! I tried to express my true feelings to family and some friends, but some of them were not able to hear me or receive what I was saying and how I felt. Instead I would I hear "he's in a better place", "God knows what best", "we can't question God", "in due time you'll move on", or "pray about it". I didn't want to hear none of that and I did not want to pray, I WANTED ANSWERS! I WAS MAD! NOT AT THE CHURCH, NOT AT MY FAMILY, NOT AT THE PEOPLE ON MY JOB, I WAS MAD AT GOD and I didn't know how to move forward from it, I had never experienced that level of resentment towards the Lord.

I didn't know where to start get over this angrier with the Lord. I felt like God took him at a pivotal point in my life, our father/daughter relationship was beautiful, we were learning so much more about each other. Laughing at each other jokes, having meaningful conversations, sharing ideas, dreams and goals for my daughter, his granddaughter. Talking about me moving forward with my life, by this time his son and I had been divorced for more than three years and he was encouraging me not to live in the past, for the future's so bright for me. Don't let my past define my future. My father in law was one of the key pillars in my transformation, in my life and now he was gone. I was like what the hell? So, I tried to pray, I ended up crying and drinking more wine till I became numb and I cried myself to sleep.

I would try to express myself to those who cared about my wellbeing and some of them would just make feel like crap and as if I had no right to be upset with God. So, I stopped talking to them about him and how I felt towards God, because sharing my true feelings with them would make me angry towards them and resentful towards them and I was already pissed off.

You see, I was blessed with two dads, my biological dad and my father in law, two awesome men that I love dearly. My biological dad taught me how to be independent, self-sufficient, a go-getter, and not to take no mess off of nobody. He taught me how to fight, to be strong and to speak my mind. My father in law taught me how to humble myself, to pray for my enemies, how to fight with prayer and fasting, how to love my enemies, how to genuinely pray for my enemies. My two dads provided me a great balance and I had the best of both worlds with them by my side.

Now it was easier and more natural for me to physically fight a person, tell a person off, cut a person off, depend on myself and get it done on my own. The challenge came practicing and implementing the tools from my father in law without feeling and being phony about it. My father in law helped me navigate through that process, that was not easy, but he was up for the challenge. Now I am sitting here drunk on my couch, crying, angry and feeling like no one is hearing me and no one understands how I feel.

As the days passed they started to feel like months and years to me, I was depleted and losing hope. Then one day a friend of mine called to check up on me. I reluctantly told her what I had been battling with over the months, I said "I sound stupid, being mad at God, don't I? But I am, and this scares me 'cause I don't know how to move forward from this." She asked me a few questions:

Sherie, have you ever been mad at your biological father?
Has he ever disappointed you, mad you upset, made you angry?

"Yes, he has."

"Ok, but you still love him, respect him, need him, care about him, and you still want him in your life, right?"
"Yes."

"When your dad made you angry, upset or disappointed you, did you share it with him?"
"Yes."

"Now, let's say you're upset or even disappointed with your biological dad about something, yet you are stranded in the middle of nowhere, you call him, tell him your situation and ask him to help you, what would your dad do?"

"He would help me"

"And, so will God. Talk to God Sherie like you would your biological dad and tell Him respectfully how you feel and then ask Him to help you. He already knows how you feel, but you haven't told Him in depth your true feelings. Tell Him, so He can help you."

God had sent my friend to call me and to guide me back Him, to move forward to Him because I had been in my own spiritual warfare. I was not mad at family, friends, colleagues, or passer-bys. I was mad at God. After that conversation, I began to pray and meditate again. I thought about what my friend said and while watching a video about overcoming grief, the speaker said, "you do not have to move on, but you can move forward remembering the love, the compassion and the knowledge that your loved one left you. You can internalize that experience and move forward with it, showing the world your loved one through you.

I sat on my couch with tears welling up in my eyes and said "I can do that" but first I have to talk to God. I didn't kneel on my knees or start off with some extravagant prayer, I sat there and began to talk to Him. I told Him I don't mean to come across as disrespectful or ungrateful, but my heart hurts, I am sad, I am angry with you and I don't want to be. I know I shouldn't be. I know you are the beginning, the end, and everything in between, but I don't know how to move forward. Please forgive me, please have mercy on me, please help me, please help my pain, please help my disappointment. I know death is a part of life, but for some reason his death has pierced through my heart like a blazing arrow that I have been walking around with and unable to extinguish the flames, my heart feels like it leaking and a bandage can't stop it. I feel numb.

I am just going through life and I need you to help me. God helped me second by second, minute by minute, hour by hour, day by day, month by month, year by year. Lord help me. After that conversation, I felt lighter and began to focus again on prayer and meditation, my attendance at church was still inconsistent, but I started to reach out and respond to church friends that had been reaching out to me and meeting up with them for coffee, lunch, and even dinner. It was baby steps, some days were better than others and some days it took every muscle in my being and prayer to move forward.

In April it will be a year since my father in law has passed away, but to be honest my life changed 12 hours after Thanksgiving dinner in 2017. From that moment to now, I learned a lot about myself, my weaknesses and my shortcomings. I experienced more lows and highs, I'd backslid, some days I felt like I could conquer the world and other days it felt like the world was conquering me.

I learned to acknowledge my feelings, address my thoughts, my emotions and take time to pause, present them to God because He said, "cast your burdens upon me." I learned to move forward, to be more authentic with myself and God. I learned that it is really okay to be me and to share my rawest feelings, thoughts, concerns, issues, and more with God. I learned not to feel ashamed or ridden with guilt, but to feel relieved that He hears me and that He will help, He will send me help, every time. I learned that "we have not, because we ask not", once I asked God for help, that was when my help came. I continue to ask God, He continues to show up, He is my source and reasons that each day I am able to move forward from the 12 hours that shifted my life and rocked my world.

Sherie Billingslea Bio

Sherie Billingslea believes that "when we are aligned to work together, the light we each bring shines brighter and stronger than the Orion's Belt." Her belief came from many trials, tribulation, disappointment, achievements, accomplishments and more.

Sherie is the founder of Brown B.O.S.S. a consulting company that provides strategic visionary coaching services to entrepreneurs seeking to enhance their brand, products, or services. She is also a believer of Jesus Christ and believes that in order for anyone to have an authentic relationship with Him, they must really be authentic with themselves. It's easier said than done, but if you put in the work you will see how marvelous He is and how you are His heir.

Chapter 15

Losing Myself, While Loving Somebody Else

I was taking away from me

By Toi Dickson-Fuller

"I AM HER"

Losing Myself, While Loving Somebody Else

I was taking away from me

I have a question to ask as you are beginning to read my story. Have you ever brought an item from the store, and when you arrived home, you notice that as you begin to put the item together a piece missing? This was my feeling about life, until I found the Lord. He has never left me, nor forsaked me.

1 Corinthians 2:9 states,

> *"Eyes has not seen, nor ear heard, Nor have entered into the heart of man The things which God has prepared for those who love him." God began to open up my eyes more and more as I prayed but I tried to run from the calling that was placed upon my life and I ran back to him in the end."*

Jeremiah 1:5

> *"Before I formed you in the womb I knew you, before you were born I set you apart; I appointed you as a prophet to the nations."*

What is Love?

You see, growing up, I've always wondered what does it mean to love yourself or somebody else? I thought this was just a word that was used in our everyday language, but really, what does it mean? No one has ever sat me

156

down to even talk about this word called, LOVE. So, I begin imitating it by watching and listening to others and it was hurting me at the same time.

1 Corinthians 13:4-5 reads

"Love is patient, love is kind. It does not envy, it does not boast, it is not proud. It does not dishonor others, it is not self-seeking, it is not easily angered, it keeps no record of wrongs."

Hi, my name is Toi Dickson. I'm 37 years old, 5ft tall and I weigh 170 pounds. I am married and I have five boys. I know as you're reading this you are probably saying to yourself why so much info already? Trust me there's a reason and you will find out why as you continue to read. I was born and raised in Cabrini Green on the Near North Side of Chicago, IL. I never thought I would reach this point, writing a book about my life. It amazes me that I've conquered a lot of challenges. I went to Schiller School, where I was somewhat popular because of my gift of singing. However, I was also teased about my face. I had bad acne. This experience made me develop some type of self-conscious about myself. I'm the only girl of 5 boys in which I have a twin brother whose name is Troy Dickson. I'm also the baby of the family. My brothers are Alex Mosley Jr., Louis Dickson, Tommy Dickson and Christopher Dickson. God has blessed me with two amazing parents, whom I love dearly. Their names are Tommie Mosley and Alex Mosley.

You know, so many of us have stories, but are afraid to share them because we don't want to be looked down upon. I know that as I'm writing my story. Some people might be able to relate. Also, I am writing my story to be able to be set free from their own discomforts. My purpose of this book is to help break generational curses that is long overdue in our families.

As I continue to write my story, I would like to say that, I'm sharing my life because it is for me to testify and help someone else overcome anything similar to what I've experienced. I am forgiving and surrendering everything over to the Lord. This has been a struggle, but something that I've made progress in my life. I am stepping out on faith (the reality of what is hoped for the proof of what is not seen Hebrews 11:1) and trust God's plan (Jeremiah 29:11 " For I know the plans I for you, declares the Lord, Plans to prosper you and not to harm you, plans to give you hope and a future.") that He has laid out for my life.

Let me set the mood for you. Right now, as I write, I am in a quiet place. It is 3:15bAM. I am in my bed writing my story while watching and hearing my one (1) year old son sleep and snoring, peacefully. There is work to be done not just for me, but for anyone who is taking the time out to read my story. God has given all of us a story to write about. That's why it's called HISTORY. When we think about things that have happened to us, we think about memories that can be either be good or bad. How we perceive how our memories made us feel is based on how we've responded to them. I encourage every woman or man to talk about your memories, so that it can help you find missing pieces to your puzzle in life; and to help you understand the person you have become today.

My Childhood Memories

As a little girl I could remember singing "I'm not your Super Woman" to my dad as he was leaving out the door for work. I don't know why I was singing this song, but it was then that my family discovered that I could sing.

As a child, I remember my mother and father working hard every day so that we would have a roof over our heads, clothes on our backs and transportation back and forth to school. Growing up we didn't have too much to complain about because both of my parents made sure that our home was first priority. My life wasn't perfect, but my parents made sure that we didn't want for anything. My mom was very over protective of us and spoke her mind about anything. My father was the total opposite, until someone made him angry.

I lived in a housing project on the Northside of Chicago, Illinois, called Cabrini Green. There were many challenges living in Cabrini Green. Because I was the only girl out of my siblings, a lot things were limited to me such as, visiting other people's house or spending the night out. When I think about it, my four brothers couldn't go far, as well. My mother feared more so for her boys because she didn't want them to be caught up in any gangs. We were involved in many programs such as CYC (Chicago Youth Centers), Cabrini Connection, Highsight and Sunshine ministries. We all attended and graduated from Schiller School and all of us graduated from High School. For high school, I received a four-year scholarship to attend an all-girl school named, St. Scholastica Academy.

Before the passing of my aunt, Louise, in 1994, she used to always take me to voice lessons with my music teacher Ms. Lena McLin. I had an amazing manager by the named, Verda Rogers. She took me on many trips such as Show Time at the Apollo; where I sang with two (2) different groups names back then FIC (Females In Control) and Pure Mahogany, and also Kim Deal (One person with many personalities.) I sure do miss these days. I signed a recording contract with Ramsey Lewis at the age fifteen (15). I was crowned Miss Teen Illinois in 1997. From there, I traveled to New York to compete against forty-nine (49) other young women from different states. I won second (2nd) runner up. I sang on a project with Kim Stratton. I continued to record songs and traveled until my manager passed away. After her passing, I began to lose so much of myself, because the fun had ended.

My mom didn't let me stop performing. She still believed in me and from there, I auditioned for the American Idol in 2001, in Chicago. I flew to California where I was challenged to select a song of my choice from the list that was that was already handpicked by the judges. It was an amazing experience, but that wasn't what God had for me. I didn't let that stop me. I continued singing. I auditioned, even with my four children television shows like, The Voice, American Idol, Sunday's Best, Chicago Idol and many more. God didn't see fit with any of those, either. During these times, God allowed the closest people around me to shift. My best friend, Sha'Meca, had to let me go in a season in my life that I didn't understand. He had to do work in her and in me. This separation left me so empty. However, still today she was and is my sister, my ride or die, my supporter and my encourager. God allowed us to come back even stronger than ever and I thank him for that. Sometimes, God will allow people around you to shift so that He can get the glory out of you!

The Dark Place Experience

The room was dark. I was sleeping on my stomach. I tried to turn over but, noticed that there was a lot of pressure on top of me. I knew who this person was, but I was so scared to move. This happened often and always at night time. There was no penetration, no nakedness, just applied pressure on my body. One time, I awakened to my hands being in a place I never consented. I never consented to any of this. I thought to myself, why would this person do such a thing to me? I didn't ask for it. I was torn into pieces as a little girl. I felt like a piece of my heart was taking away from me; especially, because we I went to tell what happened to me, this person served no repercussions.

At times I felt like a rug. A rug is used for decoration to help beautify pieces in a room. Or, it is used, sometimes for furniture to sit on top of, but after a while things build up under the rug. I felt like a rug; not the beautiful part. I felt like the dust under it. I wondered, was I wrong for mentioning this horrible feeling that happened to me? This person was protected, and I was left damaged as a young woman caring this huge burden that had never left me. This was the first day that FEAR set up within me. Growing up in the culture of my home, things were not always confronted, but yet, kept a secret.

It's time for generational curses to be broken and for people to be set FREE. I know that I am not a prisoner, but I was the victim. Now that I can clearly understand, I noticed that I still struggle with different situation. I feel that this incident has been the root to how I deal with situations I face today. First being, that when people hurt me, I don't confront them. I just find another way to avoid speaking about my hurt. I continue loving them, regardless of how they treated me. It still leaves me feeling damaged, because I'm not being to them or to myself. My second struggle is that I lost self-esteem within myself, because I have felt like this person took away part of my self-worth as a little girl. This phase in my life, I call the Phase one (1) experience. It messed me up. It is when I began to feel distance from people. I put on a pretty mask and pretended life was great. I call this phase, FEAR.

160

The ABC Experience

This experience was Phase two (2) of FEAR, because it left me hurt, lost and empty. I took away life. I really started losing more of myself.

This experience was Phase 2 of FEAR. It left me feeling hurt, lost, and empty. I really started losing more of myself during this phase.

At 15 years old, I started dating this individual that was my brother's friend. I thought he was very attractive and outgoing. And though, he was more advanced than I was, I really liked his style. He was a dancer. All of the girls were crazy about him. As we continued dating, I started sneaking doing things that I thought I was ready for. He was my first to have sexual intercourse with. Yes, he broke my virginity, at such a young age. I cried like a baby afterwards. I thought to myself, "how could I do this to myself?" I felt disgusting knowing that I had made the biggest mistake of my life. First with a condom then unprotected sex. I did not even think about the aftermath. Because, initially, it felt so good to me.

I continued sneaking around with him and one day my mom noticed me sleeping a lot. She also noticed that I was not using any of my sanitary napkins (pads). She asked me was I pregnant and not really knowing for sure I said, "No!" I was so afraid to tell my mom that I was having sex. She cared so much about my singing career not to mention I was only a freshman in High School at the time. She wanted the best for me growing up. I felt like I let her down by finding out, at 15 years old, I was pregnant.

The quickest solution was to have an abortion. My brother and mother scheduled my appointment. I couldn't voice my opinion, at all. I felt like it was a quick fix and then, I'll bounce back to life like nothing never happened.

At this time, nothing was done for my mental state of mind, either. I continued living my life. I started repeating the same cycles with a quick fix of getting rid of problems that I wanted to solve quickly. I did not think about the consequences. I took away a life that was attached to me, in two days!

I pondered on how at 4 months of my pregnancy, I could have lost my life, while getting rid of a life during a two-day procedure. I had to be dilated and that was really scary. I can remember, arriving to that place. I was nervous, scared, crying and confused. Mentally, I didn't understand what I was doing to myself. I was put to sleep and when I woke up, I was so heavily drugged that I couldn't stand up at all. I was asked by the people in the room, how was I feeling? I couldn't even respond. I felt so spaced out. I was pushed back to the room where I was initially. I was laid down in this room with other young girls and women. I couldn't stop crying because I was so heartbroken that I had just took away a life that God blessed me with. I was really beginning to feel less of myself. I knew that this was wrong to do, but I didn't have a choice growing up. Since this first experience, I've had six (6) more which equals a total of seven (7)
abortions. If you don't know, the number seven (7), biblically, represents the number of completion.

During, one of my abortion appointments I asked if I could see the end result. I was left speechless, because to see the bits and pieces that God had put together. It was so unbearable to see what a huge mistake I had made all the other times. Every time I tried to abort my other children, God always blocked it. I didn't want people to know. I was so afraid what people would think or say about me, but never considered what God thoughts were about me. I have tried to live for people but, all the while, I was so tired of living for people. This exhaustion caused me to distance myself from people even more.

For the sake of our young people please let's talk to them and not at them because it's causing them to be in unhealthy situations. I know there are many more young girls and women who have had the same experience, or who have almost had an abortion, and kept it a secret. My prayer is that it stops being a secret. No more do we have to hide the truth about our life. It happened to me and I'm not afraid anymore. My God has forgiven me.

I've made up in my mind that I will seek God in all that I do in my life and not people. My testimony has saved so many babies. I felt my mother reason behind this was to protect me being that I was so young, but I am not sure.

I even thought that maybe, she had some similar experiences, and never talked about them with people. She too may have been trying to protect them as well. Through it all my mother has never left my side and still is overprotective of me. The weight of this process has not been easy, but I thank God for my process. It was worth going through and coming out of because it helped me to realize that, God is a healer, a mind regulator, my Provider, my Protector, my Prince of peace, my first love and the Author and the Finisher of my faith.

2 Timothy 1:7

"For God gave us a spirit not of fear but of power and love and self-control."

Trials and Tribulations Make You Strong

I got pregnant, unexpectedly, in 2017. I delivered a healthy boy, that I thought about aborting as well. My C-Section experience with my fourth child in 2007, made me afraid to give birth to another child. But, God was with me and because of my commitment to Christ, I delivered another healthy and blessed baby boy. I am now a mother of five. My five kings have changed my life and I wouldn't change them for nothing in this world. But, it's been hard trying to balance myself, my marriage, my children and my job. I started losing more of myself to these daily routines. I never got a chance to live alone.

At the age of 21, I lived with my four children's father, whom I married and is still to after 16 long trying years. Being married has not been easy for me. It has been very changeling, especially, when both partners never got a chance to experience life alone before saying, I DO. So much has happened in my marriage and we both have taken the blame for it. One thing I say for sure, is before you make a commitment make sure you love yourself, know how to live by yourself and always have a conversation with the Lord before making any decisions. I love the hell out of my husband, but I feel that we both were not ready to be married, because of that many things happened. But, my God always wins in the end.

Things have started turning around for me and my family's. It has been in God's timing and I won't complain. I will continue to praise Him for his plans and not my own. I can't tell you how many times my husband and I wanted to through in the title, but GOD.

I AM HER

One day God visited me in my dream and He gave me a vision to start a business/ministry called IAMHER. He wanted me to help other young girls and women, through my story (trials, tribulations and triumphs) to be set free of any past or present hurt. I have been so amazed so amazed to see a little of what God was about to do through me. But, I didn't understand the full layout of His plan. I know as I continue to follow His plan, He will allow people to become a part of this amazing life changing journey.

After saying yes to God, this amazing man of God, Maurice Gunn, wrote a note in my birthday card. He wrote, "I'm going to make sure that 2019 is your BEST year." This was in December of 2018. I must say, that God has used him in such a powerful way to help launch, promote and support the mission and vision on IAMHER. His spoken words of encouragement, spoke life into me that day that and I needed it. The vision that God gave me for IAMHER is happening with the help of the Lord.

In all that I have gone through, I thank God that I didn't give up. Because, now, I get to help women to keep winning in life. I'm glad that through it all, I did not stop trusting or stop having faith. Even though my situations did not always look like it, I had enough faith to still believe that God would work everything out for the good of those that love him. And, I knew I loved Him (I still do). My past doesn't determine my future. I AM HER has taken off. The Lord and has changed me as a woman in so many ways. I am now confident that I've experienced enough in my life to be able to share and help others to overcome what they have held onto in their life. My gift is making room for me and it is making room for the gifts in others, as well.

My trials and tribulations used to make me feel that I wasn't enough. But, today, I encourage myself by saying that I am a woman who has a lot of wisdom, who cares so deeply for others. I am a woman who has five (5) boys, married, loves so freely and I go above and beyond to help others. I am HER; a woman who is broken before the Lord. I am stronger, and I know that I can do all things through Christ who strengthens me.

I would like to say thank you to God for allowing me to experience and endure everything that I've experienced thus far. Thanks to my mother Tommie Mosley for always being my #1 supporter in singing and never leaving my side as a mom. Thanks to my dad Alex Mosley for always being supportive as a father and taking care of your family like a man is supposed to do. Thanks to my big brother Louis Dickson for supporting me with every struggle that I've encounter and for always being honest and concerned for my well-being and my children. Thanks to my husband for supporting me with the many decisions that I've made. LOL Because it's been a lot of switching up, and I think I've found my winning one #IAMHER. Thanks to my best friend Sha'Meca Oliver; for allowing me to be a part of this amazing project that's going to help save the lives to many. Thanks to all of my family and friends who have supported me in various ways. I appreciate all of you and thank God that you all are and will be a part of this movement that He's allowing to happen. Love you -Toi

Toi Dickson-Fuller Bio

Toi Dickson-Fuller is a woman after God's own heart. She doesn't look like what she's been through. She has survived tumultuous situations, which has built her into the woman that she is today. She a loving wife, mother of five boys, of whom she calls her kings. She is youngest and the only girl of five brothers. Her soul rejoices every time she reflects about her trials, tribulations and triumphs. She remains humbly-thankful to God for sparing her life multiple times.

Toi's journey has lead her to have a passion to help others win in every area of their lives. This is why she has founded IAMHER Ministries, a not-for-profit organization that helps women and young girls overcome obstacles they have faced in life. Through IAMHER Ministries, she has created an enrichment program that she currently leads through By-The-Hand Club for Kids. She has also launched a successful IAMHER clothing and accessories line. She is committed to allowing God's light to shine in her life, so that it brings hope to the lives of many across the globe.

Chapter 16

Assassinated the Posture of Fear
- Destiny Wins-

By Dianne Raiford

"Do not look for others to push you to greatness, but allow God (your creator) to direct your paths to greatness."

Assassinated the Posture of Fear
- Destiny Wins -

"For God has not given us the spirit of fear; but of power, and of love, and of a sound mind." – 2nd Timothy 1:7

Breathe. It's, really, okay - you are free, now soar like an eagle!

Well some time ago, I could not even fathom the word "Freedom" – my thoughts, even questioned my thoughts. Freedom, what does that even look like, feel like, or can you taste "Liberty?" How did I become enslaved to my emotions? Fear, doubt, worry, insecurity, lack of confidence, looking for validation and I even used "shyness" as a security blanket.

In my younger days, by nature, I was rather reserved, but after experiencing such devastation, pain, and mistrust – my life automatically aligned itself with living in the shadow (the background), because it felt 'safe.' Although, I did share bits and pieces of my experience with a few relatives and friends, I still walked away feeling empty and always wondering whether or not they really believe me? I was constantly consumed and struggled with those thoughts, did they really believe me, and/or will they believe me?

While dating, this is where it all began, from my middle twenties to early thirties, I was molested three times by two different men. Over and over, I asked myself why did this happen to me? I did not contribute or even solicit for this type of abusive behavior. Trusting others, fear of failing, coupled with, steadily, experiencing failed relationships are hurdles that I had to overcome.

168

Gospel legendary, Johnathan McReynolds, wrote a powerful song titled" Cycles," and the lyrics speak to how to refuse going in cycles, and the song ends with the stanza "...there's power in the name of Jesus, to break every cycle..." – *A few lyrics:*

Didn't I conquer this last year?

Tell me what I missed 'cause I fear

That' it's coming back up again

Must be something I ate

Some song, some show, some hate

The devil wants to extend the game, free throws

And when it ends he want to make the sequel

'Cause if he has another chance

He feels like he can take

My joy, my peace, my faith

See the devil learns from your mistakes, even if you don't

...but when I am sure that I'm not go in cycles...there's power in the name of Jesus to break all cycles...

Breathe; *wuuuu-saaaa* - A mouthful, yes, and wow! *(smiling)*

Also, I began seeing and feeling 'my posture of power, strength, and faith' being tested, challenged and eventually becoming diluted, and I began accepting the 'posture of fear and doubt' at various times in my life. Now, it was up to me to face it, and declare over my life that it will no longer have control. But, of course instead of taking it to the altar and leaving it there, I took matters into my own hands, I tried to handle these emotions, and instead I became numb.

As life progressed, I start having short lived victories, and emotional "wins", and the wins start feeling like Facebook-watch parties, and pop-up shops. I thought this was good and I made it as my 'new normal, because I felt relieved, but really needed to slow down, stop and know that I can be rescued, restored and brought back to myself "happy go-lucky, laughing, always smiling, outgoing, and enjoying serving God."

In the midst of all of this, God was yet blessing and speaking, and the scripture that got my attention, on a Saturday morning, was *Psalms 46:10 "Be still and Know that I am God", this right here, became my private prayer, worship and bible study time.* I felt God was listening and loved me enough to deal with my emotional pain and help me start my journey of wholeness. *Hear me: John 10:10 (NIV) "The thief comes only to steal and kill and destroy; I have come that they may have life and have it to the full (more abundantly)" I am starting to see my abundance manifest – glory to God.*

Breathe! – Journal your thoughts Point #1

"Allow yourself to develop, grow and live God's plan for your life"

By D. M. Raiford

Deliverance & Restoration

You know before I got here, there was a full-fledged process – I had to be disciplined, committed in sustaining my deliverance and freedom. After turning the entire situation over to my "Creator' – God; my outlook on life began changing, and right there I decided to let go and let God *"assassinate my posture of fear", because "Destiny Wins!"*

The "Winans, "a gospel family group, recorded these lyrics - "Restoration has finally come, been restored back to my place in God." These lyrics became one of my daily affirmations, along with others. Also, my father's prayers kept me covered, along with my brother and my mom. Most times, you found us standing in the living room, just before he returned to college, we locked hands as they prayed over and for me. Nevertheless, I had to remember that I had to toughen-up, grow into my own, and ultimately have a strong committed prayer life.

Words can't describe, how I really miss hearing this voice, - Diana (dad) "your main hang up is "worrying-fearing" what others think", and of course mom, - "I don't know where she gets that from… (laughter filled the room), and at that moment, the scripture that kept ringing in my ears *"…your later days shall be greater than your former…" Job 42:12-17.* I truly thank God for all the love and support, it has now helped me stand bodily, and declare that it's time to *"Break the Silence"* and help others experience their deliverance and freedom!

While going through the process, days I felt venerable, my spiritual and natural growth were stunted, yet God's grace was enough. I thank God this was not an everyday feeling, I refocused, gained strength; my momentum start flowing, and I kept accomplishing my goals. I kept climbing the 'career' ladder without any problems, but feeling like other parts of my life were suffocating.

One of my mentors stated, stated to the group- "you do not want be broken at the top" and I concluded that day that 'wholeness' is my "New Normal." Daily, I practice and operate in my "New Normal" – "whatsoever a man thinketh, so is he" – Today, I am "Winner!" - I survived past pain and regrets, now I have submitted my will to God's will!" Definitely, this is not a buzz word for me, or something that makes me feel comfortable, but this is "my" life. - *"I wish above all that you prosper, be in health, even as your soul prospers." 3 John 1:2 - ammunition!*

When I pray and 'stand-in the gap' for souls that are stuck and struggling to breathe life, again; I immediately go into combat and rebuke that spirit and declare you shall win!

Breathe! – Journal your thoughts Point #2

"Empty yourself of all contaminations, and lock hands with wholeness"
By D. M. Raiford

_____

_____

_____

_____

_____

_____

_____

_____

_____

_____

Moving Forward

"Deliverance & Freedom" – yes, exists simultaneous! My deliverance and freedom sprung forth like a **"Tsunami"** washing all dead debris, dryness, and restoring life, but you must maintain your steady-state. I am allowing this new depth in Christ - "this well of water" which I am allowing to engulf my entire space as well as my atmosphere. And, I am ever-so grateful to be drawn deeper into the Word, and into his presence. ***Now, it's high time to live bodily for God!***

On my previous job: my co-worker and I were chatting, and somehow, we got on the subject "Living Boldly" – and she said," living bodily is me and I don't know any other way." She reminded me, just live boldly, don't allow, don't' conform to anyone's identity, and mirror their characteristics, but really know who you are, what you want out of life *and keep pushing forward to exemplify your true self.*

Well of course, I didn't go looking for a pep talk, but it came to me and it was, actually, good to sit and talk without an agenda. I told her, I remember I use to say – well, does this even look right on me, is this my personality, what are they thinking – OMG! I couldn't believe I wasted time on this craziness. And, one day, I heard a prominent person, a person of success, say "really, people are not thinking about you, in the way you even imagine." My reaction was "whew Jesus" – busted bubble!

*I said, well they show-up pretending like they do. I recognized that this was my hang-up, fear of this and fear of that, man I must have set-down, ate and kept living out a state of "Fear" – **again, it wasn't an everyday posture, because I had victories along the way, but now it's time to Win the War**.*

There's a strategic plan for winning wars (spiritual battles). Well, history is a great teacher, while looking at the 'powerful and authentic' spiritual generals in the body of Christ, and how they fought the fight of faith and how they made it through. History also tells us about lessons learned, and how not to repeat those same behaviors; even though the catastrophic events occurred in my life, I will not allow my past, dictate my future.

Your strategic plan will look different from mine, but some of the key components are: 1. Great support system, 2. Prayer, fasting and reading your bible, and 3. If you need counseling – go and get it, there's nothing with opening-up and communicating your 'painful' areas. If you don't deal with your 'painful' areas, believe me the devil will have a fill-day. So, we must not relinquish our power, but gain more strength and power. We are here to help, not place each other back into bondage with our actions, and reactions. True ministry begins when you are "Godly" equipped to minister to that spirit, through the power and anointing of God to address a person's situation.

In my new career path, "project management", there are five phases that a standard project is "tested" to go through; just imagine an intense formulated-car wash, yea I know what an analogy, but you got the picture.

The five phases are conception and initiation, planning, execution, performance/monitoring, the final recommendation report and the project closes. During the Conception (strategic planning) phase, this is where a lot of the grassroots work is done; where we are building, "gathering data, reading documents on how past projects were completed and how some failed." This just lets you know that, everything has a process, time and a season, and when that season is handled correctly, you find yourself wining "War" after "War."

I know you are saying what does all this have to do with *"Assassinating"* my or our enemy of fear. Well, I'm glad you asked, since "fear" (the enemy) is a manipulative spirit which plays on emotions and brings deliberate confusion in our atmosphere; Donald Miller, author, puts it like this, "Fear is a manipulative emotion that can trick you in living a boring life." Well said, but this wasn't my case, my life was quite happy for the most part, but I just missed great opportunities, and my steady advancement in life. So, I had to go through the "cycle "of hoping that it will come back around. Hurdling over my own disappointments and pain "waiting, again for my birthing season" to come again, "Oh boy" at times this was so unbearable.

Also, guess what, don't ever compare your season to the 4 four seasons winter, spring, summer and fall. My season and your season may feel like "winter", and it goes beyond the three month (quarter). So, just prepare and embrace your "cycle" and go through the process and make this your last 'cycle". –

Destiny Wins! - My now season is "SPRING"

Breathe! – Journal your thoughts Point #3

"Walk with integrity, talk with power, and leave with resolutions."

By D. M. Raiford

_____

_____

_____

_____

_____

_____

_____

_____

_____

_____

_____

Dianne Raiford Bio

Dianne M. Raiford is from Arlington, Virginia, who worked over 15 years in the Health and Human Service industry, which encompasses Section 8 Housing, Food Stamp Program, Transportation Department, and managing Social Services grants, and supporting region-wide block grants. She is now founder and CEO of the non-profit organizations Upward Mobility International (UMI) and MPACT (Manifested Purpose Aligned with Commitment and Truth.) Ms. Raiford loves to increase the lives of others in various ways, best results, always, allowing God to showcase them as great testimonies. She has a degree in Business Administration, Biblical Studies, Bachelors, and now pursuing her Master's in Healthcare Management, as well as certification in Program Management.

Ms. Raiford, the future "Philanthropist" is working towards another project called, "The Walls of Jerusalem" a foundation which focuses on "self-worth", building-up and encouraging each individual. This foundation links them to private, non-profit, as well as social services community-based agencies to give them hope in re-establishing their lives. This is in dedication to her father, "Mr. Louis T. Raiford and her mother, "Reverend Jeanette S. Raiford" who introduced her to entrepreneurship by establishing his own brick masonry company. In any given day, while driving through-out Northern Virginia, she sees and touches the inheritance of her father's business. Her mother was a minister in the Fire Baptized Holiness Church and has taught her the value and the importance of living a Holy life, she always encouraged all her children to "Furnishing God" a life – this meant presenting your total life as a living sacrifice unto your Creator (Romans 12:1). The center of Dianne's joy is "Prayer and Worship" in which both parents immersed her in a solid and a strong Christian foundation.

Chapter 17
SPEAK NOW

By Vickie Mclean

"God's favor is still the best Flavor"

Speak Now

I was raised in the projects of southeast, Washington, DC, in a single parent home. My Mother raised 5 children. I was the middle child. I had one older sister and one older brother, one younger sister and one younger brother. I'm sure you notice yeah, I was right in the middle. So, being raised by a single parent with five (5) kids of course, it wasn't easy. There were struggles.

My mom worked hard to keep food on the table. We didn't have a whole lot. My dad was around. He would spend the weekends with us from time to time, but financially he was unavailable. So, with having a parent to do it alone, there would come many mistakes in the lives of her kids that would happen along the way.

One of those Mistakes that happened, was me becoming pregnant at an early age. I didn't finish school on time. You see, not only did I have a child at a young age, but I had a child with Special needs. My future was looking mighty bleak! My dream was to be a "Professional." It didn't matter what kind of put professional. I just wanted to be SUCCESSFUL! My definition of being successful was being able to own a car and afford to pay rent where ever I lived. It was because of how I saw my mother. She struggled raising five children and to pay bills. Eventually, our family DC to Maryland.

My mom used to speak with her oldest daughter's father sister, who we all considered to be our aunt. She really was my oldest sisters father sister. We rented out her three (3) bed room house in Capital Heights, MD. It would be great moving there, because it is where my life would change for the better in so many ways.

See, I always imagined meeting a man who knew how to love me and my child. As time went on, I was just existing in life with no directions and very little support. I was having a hard time trying to rap my head around life. In the late 80's I met a guy, who would later become my husband. I remember walking from the corner store to get my favorite snack and a drink on this hot summer day. I was wearing a white mini skirt with a red top. I noticed a car driving pass me.

It was a Volkswagen GTI with no paint on the car. I noticed the car making a U-turn and coming back in my direction. As he got closer to me, I glanced in the vehicle and noticed he looked a little familiar. The first words that came out of his mouth was, "I know you have a boyfriend as fine as you are." So, of course I began to blush, hearing him speak of me in that way. This started our conversation. Well, as we began to talk, I realized why he looked so familiar. I remember his younger sister and I attended junior high school together. Then, we exchanged numbers and he asked me if he can drop me off at my home. I proceeded and got into his vehicle. He had a coworker of his riding in the car with him. They proceeded to take me to my home.

After a while, he began to court me. He wined and dined me. He was the first guy to surprise me with a dozen of red roses. I thought to myself, "This is how a man should be treating a lady." Not only did he wine and dine me, he also complimented me. He told me how sexy and pretty I was. We shared conversations on the phone, learning about each other and discovering that we both were single parents. That was one thing that we both had in common. He would buy for my daughter, too; which meant a lot to me. There was this one time when he gave a gift for my daughter to me and my younger brother commented, "Wow, sister, you have this guy buying your daughter things!" I thought this was flattering, especially, because he had yet to meet her. And, I had yet to share with him about my daughter and her condition. My daughter was diagnosed with having cerebral palsy; which is a whole story within itself! Sharing my daughter's condition was always a hard subject for me. Looking back over the years, I realized that I was in denial for (ten) 10 years of her life. I did not know how to truly except the fact of having a child with cerebral palsy. So, of course I was nervous sharing this with him and in the back of my mind, I wondered if he would still even be interested in getting to know me? Within a year of dating, we decided to move in our first apartment. We both were so excited getting our first place together. So, we began our life together and was married on June 2, 1994.

We were married for 19 years and there were many up and downs. You see, the man that I married, the one who came into my life and thought was my prince charming, I realized was the exact opposite. He was NOT my knight and shining armor. He was a man who was unsure of himself. He had insecurities and jealous ways; which he would allow to manifest. His jealousy and insecurity would change the outcome of us not being able to enjoy outings with family and friends. Something inside of me was saying things shouldn't be this way! I knew something was wrong with this picture. I would have to turn all my attention to him, so that our time out would not end in disappointment; all because, he can't control his emotions. I would often think, "If only he could learn to live in the moment, how better our life could be?" These kinds of thoughts would inter my mine often.

He was the same man who was loving and taught me not to pity over my daughter because of her disability. He encouraged me to treat her as a normal child. His encouragement strengthened me and helped me to become a better mother for her. He used to put me on a pedestal and would brag to his family and friends me being his wonderful wife. This man supported me financially, as a man should; as long as things were going his way. He was not be supportive of me entering the workplace, so I was a stay at home mom. When the time came for me to enter into the workplace and to have a career, there was no support for that. He was having none of that! He would always tell me that work is overrated. He would say that it's not worth the stress. He would say, "I got you baby! You don't need to work!" I would badger him over and over about how much I wanted to work. I tried to convince him to see it my way. I tried to express how it would benefit our household and it would help me begin to discover myself and have my own career. Being able to work was so important to me, because I had not completed high school yet and I didn't want to settle for any type of job. I knew I would first, have to go back to school and earn my diploma, which I finally did in 2011. I was excited when I received my high school diploma! What a very proud moment that was for me. But, he would rather work four jobs to keep me relying and depending upon him. I was dumbfounded and thought, "Why doesn't this man want me to work?" I did not realize that it was all about manipulation, power and control that he had to have at all times. What real man would not want their wife to grow in her own independence? A man who was selfish, jealous and controlling.

You see, I have been sheltered throughout my life. I was sheltered as a young girl. I was then sheltered as a married woman. Now as I look back over the 23 years That my ex took from me, I realize that he had all of those years to mold me into his ideal woman/wife. I did not realize that one day, I would not always be that naive young lady that he met 23 years ago. I would eventually take my power back! In his eyes I was pleasantly, naïve. I was unlike no other woman he ever dated in his past. Most importantly, he felt safe with me because of that very reason, naivety. You see, I wasn't materialistic. I wasn't a needy woman. So, rather than nurturing my naivety, he exploited it for his benefit. He did not allow me to become the mature women that I am today. Because of his insecurities, low self-esteem and jealousy that played a huge part of the demised, our marriage that ultimately ended in a tumultuous court battle and the fight of my life.

Our married was coming to an end. It was dysfunction and chaotic. The one thing I knew to turn to the One and only thing my grandmother show me, which was God! As far as I can remember my grandmother always live a Christian life. She was a Holy Ghost-Filled, Highly-Favored, Woman Of God! She showed me with the life she lived, how to pray and turn to God in good times and in bad times. (Oh, how I miss her. She was called home to be with the Lord.) With all the chaos that was going on in my marriage, I knew that the God I serve, is not a God of confusion. Although I was going through my storm, God hands was all over it. He was the only way I came through it all. I have learned, often, we can't find out who we truly are unless we leave bad situations that are hindering our growth spiritually, mentally, and emotionally.

The battle continued. There were multiple court dates that came about. One being for my now ex-husband to vacate the marital home, which the court gave him one week to do so. Then, within that week my ex removed everything from our home. I mean everything! Like windows, food from the refrigerator and yes, the refrigerator itself. It was not a small home either. It was a four (4) bedroom, two (2) and a half bathroom, sunroom, theater room living room, setting room, dinning room, etc. You get the point? The courts also awarded me to take ownership of the car that I had been driving for years. My ex vandalize it. He removed all four tires, radio and car bumper. I never thought that things would ever become so doomed! Mainly, because he was my husband a man who claimed to love me and would always be there for me no matter what! My life as I knew it was no more.

This chaos was followed by numerous protective orders. Then I became homeless do to my ex all-out attack on our home. Our once dream home, was now under attack. He threw motor oil all over the living room furniture and walls. You see I needed a break from all the harassment and rock throwing against my bedroom window. For once, I just wanted some peace. So, I had left to go spend the weekend with a girlfriend. Then, I then received a call from my neighbor saying, "Vickie, you might want to come check on your house because they notice water coming from the garage door." So, I drove home with anticipation not knowing what I would find. Once I turned the key to enter the home my mouth dropped in shock! It looked as if it was raining in the house. He busted all the toilet tanks while leaving the water running for days. It flooded of course! Not only that but all the doors were snatched off the hinges. "WOW!", I thought that he finally achieved his goal, which was to run me out of our home. Our dream home was unlivable NOW!

Before his final destruction of our home, there was a time when my ex called me on the phone crying, saying that he's hearing voices; just horrible things.

(When you are married to someone for 19 years you know the trouble they are in.) Because of the many sings I've witnessed over the years, I knew my husband was trouble in his spirit. So, I would encourage him to seek professional help. He would respond by saying, "No!" He felt no one could help him. Being concern for my husband, I reached out to get help for him sense he left me no option. The advice I received was, you are his wife, so you have the authority to have your husband admitted to be evaluated. Once I took control (as he saw it!) his feeling was that I threw him away. Now, I'm at a lost why is it so hard for men to seek help, especially, when it's so desperately needed. I guess it is not for me to judge.

I was awarded a divorce due to cruelty with being separated less than a year. But, God! That is all that needs to be said. Not that I'm glamorizing divorce, but God knows when enough is enough!

Vickie Mclean Bio

Vickie McLean is a survivor of a 19 years mentally abusive marriage. Employed at Target, a mother of one, Advocate in Annapolis Maryland to help pass Domestic Violence bills for Prince Georges County Maryland with former member Delegates Angela Angel Maryland House of Delegates. Volunteer at family justice center in Price Georges County Maryland. Former COO of Bound 4 Better. Encouraging other's that they too can survive. A woman after God's own heart, Completed Queen Esther Ministry held at First Baptist Church of Glenarden. Supported by Family and the host of loving Friends.

Chapter 18

Started From The Bottom, Now I'm Here

By Deona Hinton

"My peace is priceless"

Started From The Bottom, Now I'm Here

Growing in Washington DC wasn't easy. My mother and father met when they were teenagers. She attended Shaw Junior High School and he attended Langley Junior High School. Later, they attended Paul Lawrence Dunbar High School. My dad was a sharp dresser and his nickname was "Doc." He always carried a briefcase and most thought he would pursue a career as a Doctor. That's why they called him Doc. My mother on the other hand was an only girl who had 5 brothers. Both their mother and father left them when they were very small, so my Great Grandmother Bessie Johnson aka Nanny raised her and her siblings. Nanny was older, tired and couldn't do much with 6 children so my mother and several of her other siblings did not graduate from High School. She had other plans.

At the age of seventeen my mother became pregnant. Her and my dad didn't know how to tell my grandparents Albert and Jabella Hinton. After all, my grandmother Jabella didn't approve of their relationship and my grandfather was very ill. As the months went by my grandfather eventually died on February 2, 1966. He never knew that he was going to be a grandfather. I was born that August. Although my grandmother was disappointed that she loss her husband and her oldest child was now a father, she welcomed her first grandchild.

There is nothing like having a grandchild. No matter what they do it melts your heart. They can do things that you would never allow your children to do. They don't have to eat certain foods, their bedtime might be different, they can pick up things in the store and not be told to put it back, they can wet the bed and not get yelled at. These are all the things my grandmother allowed me to do. Her love was unconditional, and I was like another one of her children. After all, there was only 5 years age difference me and my Aunt Samone who is her youngest child.

At the age of two I took ill. Every morning when I woke up, I always told my dad that I was hungry. One morning I woke up and didn't want to eat. I laid around all day and as the day went on my dad said he felt in his spirit that something was wrong. As a result, he rushed me to Children's Hospital. It was located on V Street NW. When he arrived, he was told that me not being hungry didn't mean something was wrong. My dad knew his child and insisted that they examine me. They performed an examination and took bloodwork. When the bloodwork results were reviewed it stated that I had Meningitis. I was placed in Intensive Care for 21 days. In the meantime, my dad received orders from the Army to go to Vietnam. He was being drafted and his baby was in the hospital. What do you do?

My dad notified the Army that his daughter was in the hospital and he would not be able to deploy until I was released. He was allowed to stay in the US, but once I was released, he was drafted. He was gone for several years and looked totally different when he returned according to my mother. He had gained weight and was no longer he cup of tea. This was just an excuse. While the cats away the mouse will play.

We have all been in relationships and wondered if our mates were being faithful. Wondering if he or she is sleeping with your friend's, random strangers, but never your relatives. Well, while my dad was in Vietnam worrying about his child and fighting for his life my mother was having an affair with his first cousin. His first cousin was married and had no intentions on leaving his wife. He romanced her and told her everything she wanted to hear, but he never left his wife. This crushed my dad, but he managed to move on with his life. He met a classy lady named Edith Abernathy. She loved to dance, skate, play sports and was the life of the party.

Baby number two has arrived. Four years after I was born my mother gave birth to my sister Danielle. Her father was none other than my dads first cousin. This crushed my dad. He had all kinds of things running through his head. He would never be the same nor would he see women in the same light. He became bitter and angry. He fussed constantly and never smiled. I'm sure he felt like a fish that had been gutted. Not only did his first love betray him his cousin did too. Was it worth the hurt and heartache that my

187

dad and his cousin's wife Mildred felt? This wasn't a doll baby that could be returned to the store. She was here and here to stay. Although everyone loved her, she was a constant reminder of the broken trust, infidelity, heartache and pain that would never leave. My mother now had 2 children, by 2 different men, had never been married, dropped out of school and needed her own place. Although my grandmother didn't care for my mother, she was instrumental in her getting her first federal job at the Department of Labor. She was placed in a Secretarial position. My mother pretended to be grateful, but like everything else in her life she complained about the job and did just enough to get a place at 8th & H St NE and then we moved to Half Street SW in the area where the DC Baseball Stadium is now located. Having her own place was my mothers' dream, but she didn't attend to her children as a mother should. I remember sitting outside with some friends at the age of 5 and cutting my hand. I was rushed to Children's Hospital and had to get stitches. She had some friends who lived a few doors down the alley and we always went to visit. One day while the parents were downstairs doing what they did best which is be absent parents, the children were up-stairs throwing the clothes out of the window. One of the kids was downstairs catching the clothes. It was so fun. Then, on another occasion, I remember some friends and myself visiting a man who lived downstairs. You see we lived in a building that had an upstairs and downstairs unit. We lived upstairs. He was in the kitchen and we asked him what he was cooking? His response was roaches. We took off running. With all the adults who have now come forward saying they were molested during their childhood I thank God because I know he protected me.

In the early 1970's we moved to the Lincoln Westmoreland Building located on 7th Street NW between R & St Streets. This building was built from the ground up, so we felt like the Jefferson's. Moving on up. Our new place of residence was 2 blocks from Nanny's house, so my mother became even more inattentive. We spent countless hours at Nanny's house along with our cousin's Debbie, Tank and Dimples who lived with Nanny. They were my mothers' oldest brothers' children. He was an alcoholic and once he left his wife, she made him take the kids. He couldn't care for his children just like my mother because they lacked that skill. In addition, they mimicked what they saw.

Our new place was nice, and it was laid out with nice furniture. We had the beads hanging from the kitchen doorway, a record player with the fireplace at the bottom, a floor model tv and we had a color tv in our bedroom. All of these things were nice, but what we didn't receive was love, nurturing, hugs, kisses, someone who said "I love you" or a role model because different men were in and out of our household. Our place had dirty dishes in the sink, our hair was hardly ever combed, we didn't bathe regularly, we went without food at times and my mother was living her best life as if she didn't have any children.

My mother enjoyed meeting up with her men and friends. They were more important than her children. When I left Kindergarten, my teacher told my mom that I was very smart and that she should enroll me in Catholic School. She relayed this message to my dad, and they enrolled me in Holy Redeemer Catholic School on New Jersey Avenue and Pierce Streets NW. I remember my first day of school like it was yesterday. I was six years old and she walked with me to the bus stop at Florida Avenue and 7th Street NW. She informed me that today was the first and last time she would be able to catch the bus with me. From that day forward, I caught the bus to and from school by myself. In addition, I was responsible for picking my two-year-old sister, Danielle, up from the daycare center that was located on the first floor of our apartment building. Can you imagine a six-year-old catching the bus alone and having to pick up a two-year-old sibling? This was only the beginning. As the months went by there were several girls missing whose first name began with the letter D. Do you think this scared my mother and she would ask to change her work hours, arrange for someone to take me to school or see what could be done differently? No, it didn't. She sat me down and told me "if anyone ask you your name use another name that does not start with the letter D." This was hard because my name is Deona Denise. This is why they call me DeeDee.

As time went on my mother started disappearing more and more. Things got so bad that I started calling her friends to see if she was at their house. They must have said something to her because she asked me to stop calling people and she started paying me an allowance of $3.50 every 2 weeks when she got paid. This was a lot of money and I was excited. I saved my money to buy candy and do the things I enjoyed, but soon the novelty would wear off.

189

I started worrying about my mother's safety, there wasn't always food in the house, the house was filthy, and we were running the streets as if we were adults. In many instances, I felt like an adult because I was responsible for my little sister. Soon things would change.

After the countless men who lived with us, my mother would soon meet a man named Jessie Madden and marry him. Now that my mother was married, she decided that she wanted all of us to have the same name. Her and her husband illegally changed our last names to Madden. Our fathers weren't aware of the change, nor did they sign their rights away. My birth name was Deona Denise Hinton, but now at the age of nine I was now Deona Denise Madden. My classmates who had been in the same classes with me since the first grade had a hard time processing the fact that my last name was different. They asked me why my mom changed my last name and my standard answer was "she got married?" That's all I knew. She didn't sit us down to explain the change, nor did she care about how we felt. Now all of her children would have the same last name and people wouldn't know that she had kids by first cousins and out of wedlock.

We moved on up from SW (Southwest) to NW (northwest) District of Columbia(DC) and now we were on our way to Maryland(MD). My mother couldn't drive so, she didn't have a license or car. When her husband taught her how to drive, we moved to Valley Brook Apartments on County Road in District Heights, MD. Out in MD, things were not the same. When we lived in the city, we were able to visit and stay at Nanny's house. Now we were in MD and weren't near any of our relatives and my mothers' new husband used that to his advantage. They didn't get along at all so their marriage only lasted one year. Majority of the time he was missing in action. Later, she would learn that he had been creeping with someone and had got the lady pregnant. She acted as if it didn't bother her, but it did. I saw her crying a few times. Carma is a blip. What goes around comes around. Imagine putting a man you've only known for a little over one year on your children's birth certificates and changing their last names.

After their marriage ended, things got really bad. We were without food; our house was filthy, and our refrigerator was broken. Instead of my mother calling the rental office to report that our refrigerator was broken she started purchasing fast food. This didn't last long, because eating out can get expensive and she didn't make a lot. She started disappearing again. You know the usual. Men were always more important than her children. We weren't bathing again; our hair was nappy as a sheep's behind as my grandmother would say and we were without food. There was a Pizza and Burger Carryout in back of our complex. The owners new our story, so they would give us free food. When we couldn't get food from them, I stole from the High's Convenience Store. It was usually candy bars or whatever I could get my hands on. I was only 9 and we were hungry. One day we went in High's and my sister got caught. They barred us from the store. I remember being so mad with her. After all, the nearest convenience store was miles up the road. It was the 7-Eleven and it wasn't easy to steal in that store. I remember my sister saying, "I'm not like you." She never lied because I've always been in survivor mode.

With hardly any food, not clean clothes and having a mother who was always missing, we barely went to school. I remember thinking I was going to get retained in the fifth grade. I missed more days than I attended, but whenever I did return to school I could always caught on easily. It was as if I had not missed a day. My sister on the other hand struggled. She had difficulty in many subjects and my mother was always saying, "Danielle doesn't catch on like you." I didn't care and it wasn't my problem. She was never home and although it appeared as though I had assumed the role of the mother I was not. In addition, I always felt like she was my mothers favorite. I was always treated differently, and I always felt pressured. As a result, I did what I wanted to do, and I beat my sister up every chance I got.

"I received an eviction notice", this was what my mother told us. She was upset because we had been hanging in the hallways with our friends amongst other things and they evicted her. She had to find us another place to live within a short timeframe. I thought to myself "that's what she gets." If she were home tending to her children, she would know what they are doing. Instead she's out with her newest boyfriend Henry enjoying life. He had a nice place; nice car and he had no idea about my mother's past. He thought we had the same father and that our dad was her ex-husband. She never told him anything different. She believed in "Don't ask don't tell."

Our new place of residence was Kennedy Woods Apartments located on Walker Mill Road in District Heights, MD. Our living conditions were at there worst at this location. My mother started staying away from home one or more weeks at a time. I remember being so hungry and crying. We never knew when she would return home or if she planned to return at all. I remember one conversation I had with my mother because we were hungry. I called her to tell her we didn't have any food. She told me "her boyfriend wanted us to stop calling so much." This was not Henry. This was a creep who soon dumped her. I could believe what my mother had just said, and I will never forget it. The hurt and pain I felt from hearing my mother tell me to stop calling her when we were hungry. It was as if she had punched me in the gut. From that point on I knew I had to do what I had to do and that we were on our own.

For years, I had been writing and calling my grandmother secretly. I would let her know where we lived, our new telephone number and what hours to call. You see my mother got brand new when she got married. Not only did she change our last names, she moved and did not tell our dads where we lived. Oh, but things were about to change. She was tired of being a mother and wanted us to go live with our dads. We were happy to go. Where are our clothes, pack our bags, yippy? Those were our thoughts. After all, she hadn't been home consistently for quite some time.

I remember my first day at my dads house he asked me when was the last time I had taken a bath? I thought to myself "why," but I informed him that I had bathed the day before. He must have known something. I wasn't there an hour and the fireworks began. Him and his wife were arguing, and he was saying words that I had rarely heard. I tried to pretend like I was asleep, but I thought to myself "I've gone from sugar to S*&t." Over time this became the norm and my dad was always uptight. If he wasn't fussing, he was mean mugging you. Clearly, he was not happy with himself or the bad decisions he had made in his life. You see, he had followed in my mothers' footsteps. Remember Edith? She is the mother of my brothers Alvin aka Don and Kevin. Apparently, my father had been creeping with Edith's Aunt Carolyn. One day Edith came home, and my dad informed her that Carolyn was moving in so Edith and my brothers moved out. Hurt people hurt people.

From the first day until the last day, Carolyn was always trying to get me in trouble. If I forgot a spot on a dish, didn't fold a T-shirt properly or forgot to take out the trash she reported me to my father. I received a lot of beating, I stayed punished and I was truly miserable. My only saving grace was my grandmother. She knew what was going on and she disliked Carolyn. She felt like she was too old for my dad and she didn't appreciate what she had done to Edith and my brothers. My grandmother would make my father bring me up her house on the weekends, so I lived for Friday. As the weekend came to an end, I would go into a deep depression. Who wanted to go back to an environment of nonstop fussing and fighting? I hated it and I felt like I was between a rock and a hard place. I couldn't wait until August because I was only supposed to be there for the Summer.

August came and left, and I didn't hear from my mother. When I tried to call her, she had moved, quit her government job at the Department of Labor and her telephone was disconnected. All I could do was cry. Living with her was not the ideal situation, but surely living with my dad was like living in hell on earth. My friends would witness the things that I had to endure, and they would share them with their parents. Unbeknown to me, one day a Gloria Caesar's mom contacted my dad and said she needed to speak with him. She shared with him the things Gloria had seen and that she felt like I was being mistreated. He was hotter than fish grease. Not only did I get a beating, but I was punished. Why did I get punished because neighbors witnessed your foolish behavior and brought it to your attention?

She did everything in her power to keep me in trouble, but the one incident she didn't tell is when I was attacked by a young man, I knew at the age of 13. We were taking a walk and when we approached some woods, he drug me into the woods and tried to remove my clothing. At first, I thought he was playing, but I can still remember the look in his eyes and what I was wearing. Once I realized that he wasn't playing I went into defense mode. I started fighting back and somehow by the grace of God I was able to break free. I ran and as I looked back, I saw him chasing me. Little did he know I was like OJ Simpson when it came down to running. I was tall, skinny and had long legs. I put one foot in front of the other and left him like I was in the Penn Relays.

When I reached my house, Carolyn was there, and she could see the fear in my eyes. In addition, she saw all the dirt on my clothing. She asked, "where had I been and what happened to me?" I told her what happened, and she immediately asked where he lived. When my neighbor Cecelia Jacobs found out she was upset. She was dating his brother and she told him what happened. Carolyn sent word that if the young man didn't come to talk to her, she was going to inform his parents and my dad what happened. This is just one example of Carolyn's dislike for me. She didn't feel like what I had experienced warranted any therapy, justice or a conversation. If your child or step child is attacked by someone you need to call the Police. In addition, his parents and my father should have been informed. Instead, it was swept under the rug and to this day my dad never knew I was attacked.

By the age of 15, my mother had been missing for 3 years. She hadn't called, sent a gift nor visited me. One day a friend of the family named Doris Morton was shopping in Forestville Mall and she ran into my mother. She knew what I was going through so she got my mothers new number. She then passed the number on to my grandmother. My grandmother gave me the number. I remember the day I received her number I was so happy. It was as if I had hit the lottery. I also remember the fear of calling her and being rejected again. In the back of my mind I remembered that conversation where she told me to stop calling so much. I didn't let that deter me and I called. "Hello," "Can I speak to Beverly," "Speaking" and the conversation went on from there. I asked her where she lived and a thousand other questions. I was happy to speak with my mother, but I was still hurt by the fact that she had lied to me and told me that I was going to my dad's house for the summer. Not only had she lied she had carefully orchestrated her move.

All good things must come to an end and so do bad things. I had informed my mother about all of the hell I had been through. All except the attack. Somehow, I felt guilty like it was my fault. I knew it wasn't my fault, but I felt that if I hadn't gone off walking with that boy I wouldn't have been in that predicament. My mother would reveal that she now lived in Sussex Square Apartments on Brooks Drive in Suitland, MD and that I could come live with her. I was so happy, but I was terrified to tell my dad that I was living. As a result, we made a plan. I would go to school and she would meet me after school. I remember coming home and doing my choirs. My mother said "come on here. You don't have to do any choirs. You're leaving." I took what I could and left. Later, my mother called and informed my dad. If the Operator was listening to the choice words, he gave her, she got an ear full. If hc could have reached out and touched someone, I would have been it.

I'm reunited with my mother, but she has a one-bedroom apartment. We share the bed and make the best of our new living situation. At that time, I felt like anything was better than living at my dad's house. I didn't have to hear anymore fussing, cussing and look at the permanent frown on his face. Initially, everything was great. I had a boyfriend and my mother allowed him to come over. As time went on, she started acting ugly just like my father. My boyfriend wasn't allowed to come over anymore, so we started sneaking out. He would come over when she was at work. We were in love and wanted to be together, but the pressure of sneaking around and knowing she would never approve of our relationship I broke it off with him. As time went on, I came to realize that Satan was steal rearing his ugly head.

My mother's mood swings were frequent. I never knew how she was going to behave from one minute to the next. Were her and my dad related? The two of them had similar traits. They were a match made in heaven. The only difference was that she didn't curse. She kept an ugly look on her face, couldn't get along with anyone and she didn't have a permanent job. She worked with several temporary agencies and the problem always lied with someone else. She was never apologetic about anything that she did, and Danielle was still her favorite. The only difference I saw in her was that she was home permanently. She still didn't always have enough money for food so sometimes we went without meat. This was a big deal for me because there was always food in my dad's house.

With age comes wisdom about some things. I think she finally realized that those men she chased around town didn't truly want her. Some men are just dogs, but when you are the dog catcher, you have no idea. Those same men that she had placed in high regard and put before her children had walked out of her life never to be seen again. What she failed to realize is that men are not emotional beings. They can engage in sexual intercourse with many women and never connect with them emotionally. She was in the relationship for love, but they were in the relationship because of lust.

I went through so many changes living with my mother and while in the 12th grade I decided that I couldn't take it anymore. She had alienated me from my dads' side of the family, she ran my boyfriend away, she didn't want me to have friends over and I felt like a prisoner. At one point in my life I contemplated suicide. I was sick of staring at walls, I missed my grandmother and I was lonely. Instead of ending my life I decided to leave. Just like I left my father I was now going to leave my mother. I called my grandmother and told her everything that was going on and she sent my Aunt Samone the next morning to come and pick me up. We gathered up all of my clothes because I wasn't going to go through what I went through when I left my dads' house. I didn't bring any clothes and he didn't want to give them to me. He was angry and upset that I had left. Mona as we call her, took me straight to Hanover Place. I finally felt like I was at home. I was back at my grandmother's house or Mama's house. I lived here when I was born and visited a lot throughout my childhood.

Things were different now. Hanover was a place where they sold drugs 24/7. If you got out of the drug line you had to get to the back of the line. It kind of reminded me of a grocery store. I've seen folks get beat with baseball bats, folks walking naked, men standing in line to have sexual intercourse or oral sex performed on them for prices as low as $5; folks smoking crack at a young age, women 8- and 9-months pregnant standing in line for drugs, parents standing in line with their children and so much more. Although I love living on Hanover because there was never a dull moment, I had no idea what I was walking into. Had I not been strong I could have slipped into the hands of the drug dealer or started using drugs. The one thing I always knew was that I was going to be somebody. My grandmother taught me to believe in myself even when others put me down and didn't believe in me.

There were drugs everywhere with no hope in sight. I quickly realized that I needed to go to college. I had no idea what I wanted to study. I wanted to join the Navy, but just as I had finally made up my mind, I received an acceptance letter from Benjamin Franklin University in NW DC. This was an all Accounting College. I started school in September 1984. I wasn't serious about school. I just went through the motions. Every day when I returned home, I was more interested in what was going on outside than the homework assignments I had received. There was a guy named Paul aka Meatloaf who would help me with my homework. I remember him saying that if I didn't start focusing, I wasn't going to survive Accounting. Boy was he right.

I fell in love with a young man, so I thought. It was more like lust. He wasn't thinking about me. He lied and snuck around town with a young lady who was a drop out, she had a baby and her mother allowed boys to stay at their home. From what I was told, he was selling drugs out of their home and the mother was serving customers when necessary. This loser slept with me, her, her best friend and a host of other women. One day I would discover that he had contracted a sexually transmitted disease from him. I was hot, and I went looking for him. I can still see the dumb look in his eyes. We had many fist fights, arguments and once I took a rental car of his and drove all over town. Me and my girl Willette. My ride or die. He spotted us and I took him for a ride. He wanted the car back, but I refused to return it. I remember coming across the Frederick Douglass Bridge with is also known as the South Capitol Street Bridge. I was good at driving and when I loss him, I decided that we would keep the car a little while longer.

We went out to eat, to visit friends and a lot of other places because I wasn't ready to surrender the vehicle. There had been plenty of nights I had to take my Aunt Bonnie's car while she was sleep, but I didn't need it tonight. Back then we didn't have cell phones everyone had a beeper, but I didn't have one. I wasn't a drug dealer, nor did I work in an office that required me to carry one. As a result, he didn't know how to locate me. I remember us calling to find out if he as looking for us. Sure, enough he was, and he was telling folks what he was going to do when he found me. He didn't do anything because all of that pinned up anger inside of me would have unleashed a whirlwind on him. Willette didn't drive so I know she was scared to death the way I ran all over town at great speeds. If camera lights were out back, then I wouldn't have a license. When I finally got tired, I went towards my grandmother's house. Just as I pulled up, who do I see in the rear-view mirror? We got out of the car. If looks could kill.

I went from that drug dealer to several more, but I soon realized that they weren't much different. They all weren't emotionally connected to me. They appeared to only want sex and I soon realized that my future did not have them in it. This meant I had to make major changes. My cousin Shirley Hopkins got me my first job at the National Institutes of Health (NIH) in 1985. The following year I met my kids' father, Andre' Cluff. How we met was truly funny. He thought my name was Michelle. That was my coworker and friends name. We used to tease Michelle about him until I saw him in the hallway, and he called me Michelle. I quickly corrected him, and I went and told Michelle that he called me her. She laughed and said, "It's you that he likes."

Later that week, we went on our first date. When he called me to confirm, I pretended like I wasn't hungry. He said, "come on, I thought we were going to dinner?" I agreed to meet him at the Red Lobster in New Carrollton, MD. When we arrived, I pretended to be shy and that I wasn't hungry. You know that old saying "When you tell one lie you have to tell two?" When the food arrived, he sat back and observed me. I didn't even realize it. When I finally stopped eating, he chuckled and said, "I thought you weren't hungry?" I was embarrassed, but I played it off by laughing. We continued our evening eating and talking about our jobs and the things we had experienced as Native Washingtonians.

After that first date, I couldn't shake him. He wanted to see me daily. One day he popped up at my house and told my grandmother that he was taking me with him. She said to me "you know what to do." I thought to myself "Lady are you selling me off to this stranger." We left the house and went to the movies. I will never forget the time we went to the movies on another occasion and I was driving my 1985 Nissan Maxima with my sunroof open. My dad had given me this as a birthday present for my 19th birthday. I told him I wanted a car and if I didn't get it, I was through with him. That car was parked outside. During our stroll to the movies a bird pooped in my hair. I was loss for words. We were in route to the movies on New Hampshire Ave near University Boulevard and I had to stop by my cousin Shirley's house to wash my hair. I was so embarrassed. I was not used to washing my hair because I kept a standing weekly appointment with my hairstylist, Wanda Freeman. All I could hear was my grandmother saying to me, "Your hair is so nappy who in the hell is your Pappy lol." She used to always say that to me, and we would laugh.

As time went on, we grew closer, but we always seemed to argue. I watched my dad talk to women in a disrespectful manner and as an adult, I was determined that no man would holler, curse or disrespect me. When I met big Andre as I will refer to him in this chapter, I did not use profanity. I always felt it was not lady like. As time went on, I learned to curse like a sailor. I'll never forget the day my first cousin Tony Lewis asked me "DeeDee when did you start cursing?" I had never used such vulgar language, but this man brought out the worse in me.

In 1988, we had our first child. Andre' Cluff Jr. Our son was born prematurely and only wore 2 pounds and 4.5 ounces. Before giving birth, I asked the Doctor "if my baby was going to live." His response was "he couldn't guarantee that I would live because my blood pressure was so high, and I might go into a comma." In addition, he stated that "he wasn't going to be able to give me much anesthesia." He said, "I will probably feel everything." He didn't lie because I hollered during birth from that knife cutting me until I passed out. I woke up in Intensive Care where I remained for 3 days. My baby was so small that I could hold him in the palm of my hand. I'll never forget the first time I saw him. He had tubes in his nose, an IV in his arm and there wasn't any sound coming out when he cried. He remained in the Neonatal Unit for 2 months. In 1990 we had our second child which was another boy. He decided we would name him Allante' Cluff. For years we tried to have a girl, but nothing happened. In 1995, she finally arrived, and he decided we would name her Alon Cluff.

Although we had children, a house, nice cars and everything I had always dreamed of I wasn't happy. We constantly fussed, and I felt he was jealous of the love I showed the children and how I strived to have a better life for my family. During this time, I was enrolled in the University of the District of Columbia (UDC) working towards my bachelor's degree in business management. In addition, I had 4 jobs. He would always say "if you leave me no man will want you with 3 kids." I listened to that for years. Not that I believed it, but I tolerated it so that I could accomplish my goals. Not realizing that it made me bitter and angry. I was already an emotional wreck from all of the things I experienced throughout my childhood. I learned to tolerate people and situations. I saw myself turning into an angry person just like my mother and father. It was learned behavior. I was always made for no reason and I wasn't afraid to show it.

One day after getting my hair done by my girlfriend Vertinia at her house I returned home with the kids. When I arrived, an argument ensued. Things got ugly and I decided that this was it. I went upstairs and grab a few things and decided I was never going to return. I had my one-year old daughter on my hips, Allante' was 6 and Andre' was 8. I'll never forget he told me to "get out" and he kicked me in my butt with the baby on my hip as I exited our home. I could have fallen, but he was unbothered. Not to mention, this was not his home it was our home. I called my grandmother and she said to bring the kids and come home.

When we arrived at 39 Hanover Place, my grandmother told me to take her room which use to be my room when I was a teenager. It was the biggest room in the house. I had the kids sleep in her bed and I slept in a recliner for 1 ½ years while finishing up my degree at UDC and working those 4 jobs. I worked at NIH full time, Linen N' Things part-time, UDC as a Testing Administrator part-time and at ARE as a Youth Counselor. I don't know how I did it, but I worked 7 days a week and managed to squeeze school in too. Some days I was so tired that I felt like I wanted to pass out. I couldn't get sick because my kids needed me, and I had to purchase every all over again. Our house went into foreclosure, but I didn't care because I was free. I no longer had to endure that mental and emotional abuse. Material things come and go, but my sanity was not guaranteed.

In January 1998, we moved into Washington View Apartments on Stanton Rd SE. I explained to the Manager that my credit was bad because I loss my house. I told her everything I had to endure while being in a relationship with my kids' father. She reviewed my credit report and stated she saw where everything fell apart for me at one time. She then stated that I was approved for the apartment and no security deposit was required. I jumped for joy. While working at Linen N Things I befriended a gentleman named Mohammed. He also worked as a Manager at Levitz. Mohammed informed me that I could come to the store and pick out whatever I wanted, and he would allow me to use his discount. I picked out some nice furniture and it didn't cost me a fortune. My Uncle Gregory aka Wild Bill, went and picked it up for me. He brought the furniture to my new apartment and assembled every piece. I was overjoyed and grateful for every person who had assisted me while on my journey. There were so many people who believed in me and I wasn't about to let them down.

I continued to work 3 part-time jobs initially, but eventually I only had one part-time job. We remained in our apartment for 5 years. In 2002, my sister informed me that she was going through a housing program called NACA and that I was going too. I stated that I wasn't ready to be a home owner again. She informed me that the interest rates were down and now was the time to buy. I registered and went to the mandatory seminar with her. In September, I purchased my second home. When you purchase a home "there is no place like home."

In December 2002, I went to the Giant on Campus Way South in Upper Marlboro and ran into my high school sweetheart. He asked me for my number, and we started dating. I should have known this relationship was not what God wanted for me, but I continued seeing him because we always had a good time together and he wasn't disrespectful. Over time Satan would rear his ugly head. He started coming up missing and I noticed a change in this behavior. I couldn't pinpoint what was going on, but I knew something wasn't right. Later, he revealed that he had a substance abuse problem. I thought to myself "Dee you sure do know how to pick them." This relationship took me on a roller coaster ride.

We were off and on for years since he was a substance abuser. I had seen many people in my lifetime use drugs so, it didn't bother me like it would most. The thing that I made clear to him was if he ever brought that drama or the things that come with it to my house, I would end the relationship. He understood my loud and clear, but he had difficulty keeping a job. One day while we were sitting down having a conversation, I asked him what type of job would make him happy. He stated, "he enjoyed driving trucks." After all, when I met him, he already had his Commercial Driver's License (CDL) Learners Permit. He just needed to get the license. Our friend Willie Peoples aka Boxcar and Darren Smith aka Smitty assisted him with learning all the aspects of dump trucks so that he could pass the driving test. He took the test and passed.

Initially, when he first received his CDL he drove for several companies, but he would get terminated or quit for one reason or another. I eventually decided that I was going to make this situation work for me and him. I borrowed money from my Thrift Savings Plan (TSP) and started my trucking company in August 2005. I hired him as a driver and that very next year I was awarded 3 contracts. All totally over $2 million dollars. I was elated. I then decided that I needed new equipment, so I took my contracts to the dealership and purchased 2 new dump trucks. 4 months later I purchased 2 more new dump trucks. A short while later I purchased a used dump truck. This brought my fleet up to 5 dump trucks. I was happy and God showed me what He could do for me. Every week I received six figure checks. Although all the funds did not belong to me; a large percentage was mine. I was overjoyed. My monthly company expenses were around $50k and I was never late paying a bill.

In November 2006, we got married. He thought he was everyone's boss and I received complaints from my employee's; which included the subcontractors and the vendors I dealt with daily. It was his drug addiction, but he couldn't see it. The more money the company produced the worse he got. Eventually, he started cheating. One Friday night, in September, me and my daughter Alon went to my yard in Upper Marlboro where I parked my trucks. I noticed his car in the cut. As I pulled up, I noticed a young lady on the passenger side of his pickup. I immediately jumped out of the car and opened his car door. I didn't realize that my baby girl had went to the other side of the vehicle and was about to fight the lady on the passenger side. I looked down and hit my husband in the head with an object in the truck and then I grabbed my daughter who was chasing the lady whose name was April to her car. My daughter called her all kinds of names. She using words I would never say. I gave my life to Christ in 1999 and hadn't used those type of words since. After she chased the lady off, she came over to the driver side and wanted to fight my husband. It was at that moment I realized that this marriage was not going to work. My daughter was out of character and if this was an example of what was to come, I didn't want nor did I need that. I'm supposed to be a positive role model.

I put my husband out and did my detective work to get April's number. I informed her that I would inform her husband about what I witnessed if she ever returned to my yard. In addition, I explained that I was nice on that day, but if she returned, she might not make it out the yard. April acted like a big bad wolf on the phone, but when I invited to come back, she didn't show.

In the coming months I reconciled with my husband and forgave him. I tried to put the incident behind, but my kids wouldn't let it go. I'll never forget the day my daughter called me to say she overheard my husband on the phone talking to a friend and what he was discussing. I called him and told him not to be at my house when I returned. This back and forth went on for years. He stole fuel from me, took side jobs with the trucks, but I always found out because no one liked him, and everyone loved me. If that saying, "snitchers get stiches would apply here a lot of folks would have stiches." One day I woke up and decided this was it. I ended up in the hospital and an embarrassing conversation with a Doctor let me know he did not value his life nor mine. I waited until he got in the shower and took his keys off the keyring. He never knew they were missing. He left out for work and I smile like nothing was wrong. When he returned, he noticed he didn't have his keys on the ring. I packed his clothes and took them to his mother's house. There is always a return policy even if it is written in fine print.

In 2013, I retained a Lawyer and filed for a divorce. The divorce was ugly because as my Aunt Bonnie always says, "the people you marry are not the people you divorce." In the end I did a settlement agreement because it was best for me and my situation. He walked away with several things but was he happy? I know I was because it was at that moment I knew "my peace is priceless." Being in a relationship with him I was never going to be happy. In May 2014, we were granted a divorce and I closed that chapter in my life. I waited months before I started dating. After all, I was separated for 2 years while married to him and I did not talk to a soul. I valued my covenant with God, and I wasn't breaking it for anyone. Later that year I started going on dates, but nothing materialized. Most people only wanted sexual relationships or that was a requirement and I wasn't willing to do that.

In January 2017, Sha'Meca Oliver had a vision board party. Me and several of my friend's attended the party. It was different because we cut out pictures and words to put on our canvas boards. We were also allowed to paint items on the board. I'm no Artist so I cut and paste everything. One of the main visions I had for myself was to get married again. I posted a picture of Edris Elba on my board with hopes of finding me a handsome man like him. I continued to go on several dates even leaving one date at an event. He couldn't believe I had left, but I had. I felt like Beyoncé "You must not know my name." After that incident, he knew what he could and could not do with me. I wasn't going to be disrespected and treated like most women. I had experienced that on too many occasions, and I knew my worth. I knew enough to know that when you do something different you get something different.

In April 2018, my daughter decided that she wanted to move into a house I purchased for her when she was 17 but was too young to move into it. She needed furniture which included a mattress. She asked about an old family friend named Gerry who was a good friend of my Uncle Boo for over 30 years. My Uncle Boo had died recently so I had to get the number from his daughter Kim. She gave me the number and I called Gerry to see about a mattress. When I called, he did not answer so I left a message. He must have been screening calls because shortly thereafter he returned my call. When I answered the call, he gave his condolences and I explained why I called. He then informed me that he no longer worked, but he did have a mattress connection. After we talked about the mattress our conversation evolved about us, our past and what we wanted in our future. We talked for 1 ½ hours. At the end of the conversation, he asked me to go to dinner with him. I agreed, and we met at the Olive Garden at Ritchie Station. I didn't eat because I was doing an intermittent fast, but the conversation was good. At the end of the night we decided that we wanted to see one another.

As our journey began, I first explained to Gerry that I was practicing celibacy and if he couldn't deal with that the relationship would not move forward. He stated that he would respect my wishes. My thoughts have always been that sex blinds us especially women. We get emotional and fall in love. The man might not even love nor want us, but because he has had intercourse with us, we believe we are now a couple. He might just be trying to release stress with no intentions on being in a relationship with you or anyone else. Have you ever heard that old saying "been there done that?" That's how I felt. I've been in relationships with guys and had sex before marriage and nothing good ever came out of those relationships. In addition, I knew that it was wrong, and it was not what God wanted for me. I had given my life to Christ, but was I truly living my life for him. This was one of the areas I needed to work on. I had to examine myself from the inside out and I didn't need any blinders to get in the way. It's like watching a 3D movie where you need glasses to truly see what's coming at you.

As time went on, we started praying together, discussing the bible, we went on dates every Friday and I knew God had sent this man to me. I made my request on my vision board and it finally came to Fruition. We had early morning and late-night conversations and each time they ended, I wanted more. Every time we were together, I wanted to jump in his arms and tell him about the joy I felt inside. Well he must have felt the same way because after about 6 months he asked me to marry him. I said yes, but I told him he had to ask my dad. He looked at me as if I had asked him to jump off the 14th Street Bridge. He has known my dad for years and he knew he was up against a real challenge.

In December 2018, my dad turned 70 and we along with other family members took my dad to lunch. During lunch Gerry asked my dad to marry me and he said yes. No one at the table heard their conversation, but boy was I happy and it felt like a burden had been lifted off my shoulders. At my age many might think "why does she need her dad's permission." It is out of respect and before a wedding ceremony the parents walk in before the bride and have authority. Once the father gives the bride away, they no longer have authority over the bride, and they walk out behind the couple who are now one flesh. On May 4, 2019, I am getting married to the love of my life Mr. Gerry Leon Chambers. Although I've been in many relationships and had many ups and downs, I know that God brought us together because we are meant for one another. Proverbs 18: 22 states "He who finds a wife finds what is good and receives favor from the Lord." I thank God he found me, and I know that the favor of God is on our lives. We will always keep God first in our lives.

Deona Hinton Bio

"Business Coach"

Deona Hinton inspires people to win! Growing up, she saw that the odds were against her. Being raised in an unorthodox home and in an underprivileged community, she understood that if she kept the same mindset, she would be a product of her environment. Deona decided that she was going to challenge herself and beat the odds. She had to sacrifice and save so that she could have financial security and teach others how to do the same. As a young woman and mother of three, she committed her skills and expertise as a valued employee to a corporation. She is the owner of a female minority owned business called, Denang's Trucking, LLC. With over 33+ years of business operations experience, $3.4 Million Dollars in contracts. Deona is passionate and dedicated to empowering others to be Healthy and Wealthy. She understands that anyone can start from the bottom and rise to the top! Business Coach, Deona Hinton, has launched her course called, "How to Start A Winning Business"; providing business owners with a roadmap to maintaining a winning business.

Facebook: DeeDee Hinton IG: live_healthy_travel_wealthy

Ready To Write Your Story?

These courageously-bold women have broken their silence, by owning their power and sharing their truth, will you do it, too?

Your Voice and Your Story Matters

It is liberating to break free from the things that have kept us bound. Not only does it provide healing for those whom we share our story with, but the process, provides healing for us as well. Are you ready to be bold and share your truth, to help someone else do the same?

If you know that this is your time to allow your voice to be heard and your story to be told,
and you want more information about how you can be a co-author for the next Breaking The Code of Silence, Now!, email:
BuildingTheBestYou@iamshamecalatai.com

Sha'Meca Latai' Oliver
Visionary, Breaking The Code of Silence, Now!

Breaking The Code of Silence, Now!

Chihauna Hunter Email: Shetreasures18@yahoo.com FB: Chihauna Hunter IG: Shetreasure_bracelets_things Websites: Shetreasure.com & www.etsy.com/shop/SheTreasure	**Lisa Matthews** FB: L Arnaz Matthews @LisaMatt1128 Twitter/IG: L Arnaz Matthews Email: familyadvocatedc1@gmail.com	**Shay Lewis-Sisco** FB: @iamshayspeaks FB: Shay Divine Sisco IG: @iamshayspeaks YouTube: @iamshayspeaks E-mail: shayspeaks1@gmail.com Website: www.iamshayspeaks.com https://www.linkedin.com/in/iamshayspeaks
Danielle Fee Vaughn FB:Danielle Fee Vaughn FB: @danikeyscoaching IG: @danikeyscoaching Email: Dani@danikeys.org Web: www.danikeys.org	**Melinda Chervil Cobb** FB: cobb hairbraidingteacher Melinda FB: nywele salon, incorporated	**Sherie Billingslea** IG: @brown_b.o.s.s FB: Brown BOSS Twitter: @_BrownBOSS Email: info@thebrownbosstakeover.com Web: www.thebrownbosstakeover.com
Deona Hinton-Chambers Email: denangtrucking@gmail.com FB: DeeDee Hinton IG: Live_Healthy_Travel_Wealhy	Nicole Smith IG: @Bulafit_with_Nicole	**Toi Dickson-Fuller** IG: Iamher729 FB: Toi Dickson-fuller Email: IAMHERMINISTRIES78@gmail.com
DeShanta Hinton FB: DeShanta Hinton IG: @prettynic0le1 Email: faithalwaysworking2000@yahoo.com	**Patricia (Shay) Cosey** FB: Shay Cosey IG: Shay_Beauty YouTube: ShayBeauty	Tyra Lane-Kingsland FB: @inspiredfully IG: @inspiredfully Web: www.inspiredtolivefully.com
Dianne Raiford Dianne Raiford: IG @smiles_dmr, FB: Dianne Raiford, FB: UMI LLC Philanthropy, email: umillc18@gmail.com, website: https://umillc18.site123.me/	**Regina Franklin** Email: Msgina1024@yahoo.com IG: @Msgina1024 FB: Regina Anderson-Franklin	Veronica Howard Email: Howardveronica41@yahoo.com Fb: ReneestartinganewHoward
LaDonna D. Mitchell IG: @career_quake FB: LaDonna D. Mitchell FB: CareerQuake Email: careerquake@outlook.com Web: https://ladonna-obafemi- ne.wixsite.com/careerquake	**Rev. Dr. Rene Minter** FB: Dr-Rene Minter IG: Dr Rene Minter DMin, LCSW-R Twitter: Dr. Rene Minter LinkedIn: Dr. Rene Minter DMin, LCSW-R Email: Rmintercarr@msn.com	Vickie McLean FB: Vickie McLean Email: Vickie.mcghee@yahoo.com

About The Visionary

Sha'Meca Latai' Oliver, The "Root Coach", Girl Code Extraordinaire, Pastor and International Spokeswoman. She gets you to the root of your issues, brings her expertise in empowering women and brings it all together with the Word of God. She knows that one of the best ways to lead someone is to, "Live What You Teach." Her passion and voice to build others stems from her personal time of isolation and rejection. From these experiences, Sha'Meca has learned that women grow and thrive when in a supportive community; therefore, she has committed to walking alongside women so that they won't have to "do life" alone.

She is a believer, wife to Wesley Oliver, and mother of four children (XI'-Sairity, SeLacious, Chayim and YaPheniya). Sha'Meca is the CEO of Building The Best You, LLC; which creates spaces, opportunities and platforms for women who lead, to be healed and successful. She is the founder of Pneuma Breathe Ministries, whose purpose is to Reach, Train and Transform the lives of others through the wisdom and power of God. She is also the founder of Daughter to Daughter Women Chapters and Mentorship Program. As the creator and host of the "Building The Best You" show, Sha'Meca spotlights individuals who've exemplified trials to triumphant living. These testimonies serve to show the next woman, that she too, can be healed and successful. Her entrepreneurial spirit was cultivated by her parents, who encouraged her to always dream, create and pursue. With their support she has inspired many through dance, acting, performing off-broadway and touring internationally. And, in keeping with her passion to build the next woman, she authored the book, "Believe You Can", a blueprint for getting started and finishing anything.

Stay Connected

Sha'Meca Latai' Oliver
IG: @iamshamecalatai
FB: Sha'Meca Oliver
FB: Building The Best You
Email: Buildingthebestyou@iamshamecalatai.com
Web: www.iamshamecalatai.com

Made in the USA
Middletown, DE
24 June 2019